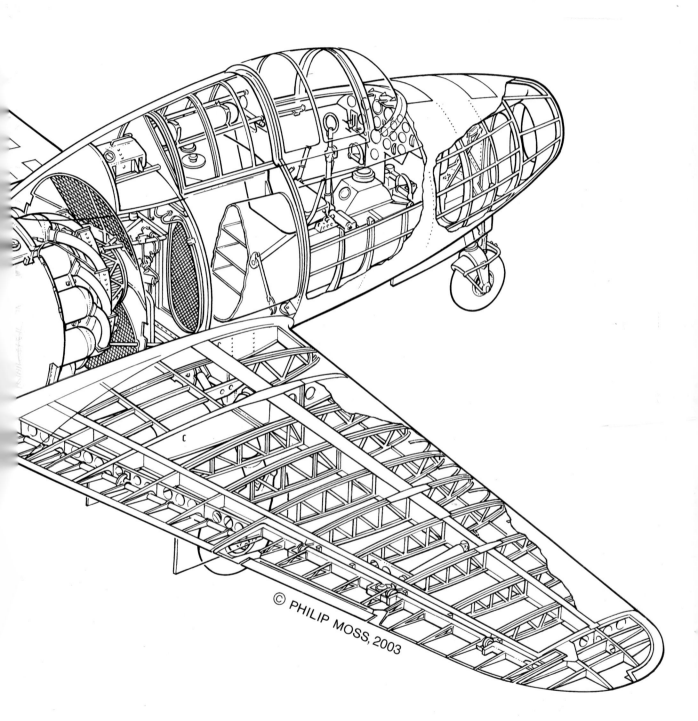

© PHILIP MOSS, 2003

JET
PIONEERS
GLOSTER
AND THE BIRTH OF THE JET AGE

TIM KERSHAW

SUTTON PUBLISHING

First published in 2004 by
Sutton Publishing Limited · Phoenix Mill
Thrupp · Stroud · Gloucestershire · GL5 2BU

British Library Cataloguing in Publication Data
A catalogue record for this book is available from the British Library.

ISBN 0-7509-3212-0

Typeset in 10.5/13.5pt Photina.
Typesetting and origination by
Sutton Publishing Limited.
Printed in Great Britain by
J.H. Haynes and Co. Ltd, Sparkford.

CONTENTS

*In memory of Wilfred George Carter CBE FRAeS,
1889–1969,
aircraft designer and jet pioneer*

FOREWORD

This is the historic story of Britain's first jet-propelled aircraft, the Gloster E28/39, and its designer, George Carter. It spans a wide spectrum of the aviation scene in this country from 1914 to 1948, and inevitably it projects the names of many famous aircraft and personalities of that golden era in aeronautics.

The birth of the E28 was the result of the somewhat random selection of the Gloster Aircraft Company to design and build a vehicle to accommodate jet pioneer Frank Whittle's first flight engine. Fortune smiled on this arrangement, for it brought together two kindred spirits in Whittle and Carter. The saga of conducting such a project in utmost secrecy in wartime conditions makes enthralling reading, and involves almost in parallel the evolution of Britain's first operational twin-jet Meteor fighter from the same stable.

The biographical insight into George Carter reveals a good team man, who quietly inspired loyalty from his workers on the shop floor through to his test pilots in the air. The book is indeed a fitting tribute to a modest but superb engineer, and to the pioneering aeroplane he helped to create.

I had the great good fortune to know both man and machine, as well as the mighty Frank Whittle, and experience the thrill and privilege of working with such unforgettable engineers and the products of their genius.

Capt Eric Brown CBE DSC AFC MA FRAeS RN
Former Commanding Officer High Speed Flight and Aerodynamics Flight,
Royal Aircraft Establishment, Farnborough

The earliest photograph of the Gloster E28/39: the monocoque skeleton takes shape in the Gloster Aircraft Company's Experimental Department in August 1940. *(© Crown Copyright/MOD)*

ACKNOWLEDGEMENTS

Many individuals and organisations have made this book possible, but above all I could not have considered embarking on the project without the resources and contacts of Jet Age Museum. I owe a particular debt of gratitude to the management and members of Jet Age.

I am also especially grateful to the family of George Carter, to his son, Peter, for allowing me to dedicate this book to his father's memory and to quote from his father's work, and to Peter's cousins Sylvia McGhie and Pauline Watson for all their help and encouragement. Thanks, too, to John Patterson for his help with Carter family contacts.

Outstanding contributions to the illustrations in this book were made by Roff T. Jones, saviour of the E28 construction photographs, and Valerie Adams, whose late husband, Russell Adams, was the undoubted pioneer of jet air-to-air photography. The Russell Adams Collection is a fantastic resource and I am delighted that it is now under the management of Jet Age Museum for the joint benefit of the Museum and Russell's family. I am also grateful to the Crown Copyright Administrator of the Ministry of Defence for permission to publish many photographs, especially those saved by Roff Jones; to Michael S. Daunt for permission to use photographs from his father's collection; and to Roger Jackson for photographs from the A.J. Jackson Collection.

Thanks, too, to technical illustrator Philip Moss and aviation historian Tony Buttler, two Jet Age Museum stalwarts. Thanks to Phil for his outstanding cutaway drawing of the E28, which I believe to be the first of its kind. There simply was not enough information available before to show the E28's insides. It has been made possible by access to the original glass plate negatives of the company's general arrangement drawings, the once-secret Prototype Notes and the construction photographs referred to above. And thanks to Tony for sharing the fruits of his impressive research at the Public Record Office (now the National Archives) on early Gloster jets, for the loan of photographs and for his tremendous support throughout.

Eyewitness accounts and records have been contributed above all by Sid Dix, Dr Robert Feilden and Capt Eric Brown RN. Dix and Feilden saw the E28 leave the ground at Brockworth on 8 April 1941, and all three were present at the first flight at Cranwell in the following month. Sid Dix is the last survivor of the team which built the two E28s; Bob Feilden is a distinguished former member of Frank Whittle's Power Jets team who supervised the installation of the engine for the first taxiing trials; and Eric Brown is the last survivor of the twenty-five men who flew the two aircraft. I am also especially grateful to Eric Brown for his foreword.

Thanks, too, to Ian Whittle for permission to quote his father's words from various sources, to A.K. Walker and John Walker for access to the late Richard Walker's notes and photographs, and to Brian Riddle of the Royal Aeronautical Society. I have also drawn on Jet Age Museum archive material from former Gloster personnel Bill Baldwin, Basil Fielding, John Cuss and Sidney Hill. Other contributions have come from correspondence or conversations over the years with Janet Ashton, Les Comfort, Michael S. Daunt, Roff T. Jones, Cyril Richardson, Maurice Summers, Joe Tedaldi, Don Tombs and John Whitaker.

Published sources have been used extensively to provide the main narrative. I have relied in particular on Gloster test pilot John Grierson's classic, *Jet Flight* of 1946. Many other sources have been used, both published and unpublished, and they are listed in the bibliography.

Help and encouragement have made this book possible and I am especially grateful to Jet Age Museum chairman John Lewer, my editor Sarah Bryce and the Sutton Publishing team (Clare Jackson, Bow Watkinson, Michelle Tilling, Joanne Govier, Mary Critchley, Catherine Watson and Martin Latham), my wife Nicky and my daughter Kate. Thank you all. Writing the book would have been far harder without your support.

While every effort has been made to obtain copyright clearance and consent, if I have missed anyone I would very much like to hear from them so that I can put this right. Finally, I would like to make it clear that any errors are my own and any corrections or new information will be gratefully received.

INTRODUCTION

J et flight has changed the world we live in, as surely as the telephone, the car or the internet. Each of them has expanded the network of communications which links us all. Powered flight has been with us for a hundred years: we celebrated the centenary of the Wright brothers' first flight in 2003. Their Flyer was powered by a petrol engine driving twin propellers. This combination of internal combustion engine and propeller prevailed for forty years or more, with increasing power and sophistication, but it had its limitations – and they were recognised as far back as 1928 by a young Royal Air Force cadet named Frank Whittle. His dogged determination and the essential rightness of his vision produced a quantum leap in aircraft performance unlike anything before or since.

Whittle is honoured today as a true British engineering genius and the outstanding pioneer of jet-powered flight. His achievement is well known and the development of the jet engine has been covered thoroughly in print and documentary. This book looks at part of the story from a different angle: the part played by the people of the Gloster Aircraft Company in designing, building and flying the first aeroplane in which Whittle's revolutionary invention took to the air. It looks at how and why the company became involved in this extraordinary project.

When I was approached to write this book I wondered what I could add to previously published accounts and how on earth I could find enough illustrations. In the event, I was able to find a remarkable amount of new material, including eyewitness accounts and anecdotes, and once-secret documents and photographs. I have also gathered together scraps of information from a wide variety of sources. No one before had attempted, as far as I know, to cover the career of aircraft designer George Carter in any detail, or to assess his place in local and aviation history. I have pieced together fuller accounts than I have been able to find from any other single source of the careers of Richard Walker and the four Gloster test pilots who flew the E28. I have also tried as far as possible to do justice to the many other Gloster personnel who were involved in the project.

Most remarkable and noteworthy of the new material is the extraordinary collection of photographs of Britain's first jet being built. As far as I am aware, this remarkable record has not been published before. Now, for the first time in more than sixty years, they see the light of day once more. The month in which each was taken is recorded, so we have a good idea of the rate of progress that was made in building the E28s, although it is not always clear which of the two aircraft is depicted.

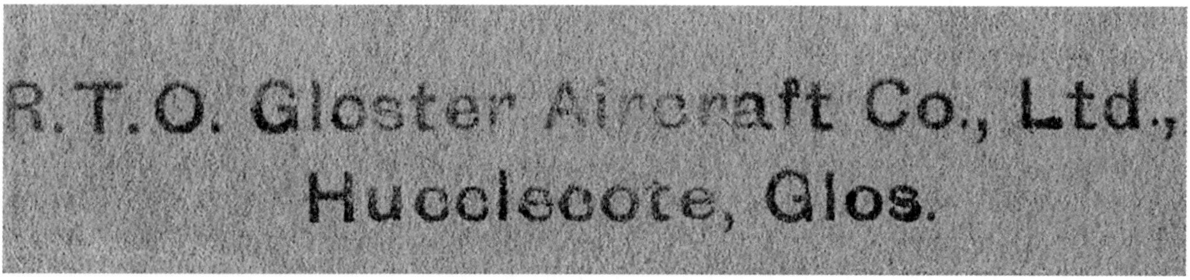

The rubber stamp inside the rescued album of E28 photographs shows that it belonged to the Resident Technical Officer, Bill Yardley. *(Roff T. Jones)*

The survival of the photographs is an extraordinary story in itself. There are 110 in all, of which, I believe, no more than half a dozen are well known. The full set – all with SECRET stamped on the reverse – was pasted into an album issued by the Gloster Aircraft Company Stationery Department and each page is stamped 'RTO Gloster Aircraft Co. Ltd, Hucclecote, Glos'. The RTO was the resident technical officer, the Air Ministry's permanent representative with the company.

The album found its way in due course to the bottom of a filing cabinet drawer where it languished until the company closed down in 1963. Designer Roff T. Jones was the last man out of the design office. He was told that two lorries would come from Coventry to take the design office records away; it was his job to supervise the loading. For whatever reason, only one lorry arrived. Jones was told to take everything that was left to the bottom of the airfield and burn it. Before doing so he looked to see what was about to be destroyed. There was the photograph album, which he kept safe for forty years.

Tim Kershaw
Bushley, Tewkesbury
February 2004

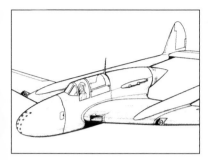

WHY GLOSTER?

Unable to attract official support, Frank Whittle found enough private backing to set up a company, Power Jets Ltd, in 1936 to build a prototype gas turbine engine – a 'jet'. In April the following year his U-type engine was successfully run for the first time – the first time, indeed, that a jet engine intended for flight had run anywhere in the world.

The Air Ministry, indifferent if not downright sceptical for so long, began cautiously to take notice. Whittle had gone beyond theory, surmounted a host of daunting technical challenges and shown that the thing could work. This was a time when it was commonly and widely believed that the future of air power lay in bombing the enemy's factories, infrastructure and population centres, that there was no effective defence against bombing aircraft en masse and that 'the bomber will always get through'.

When it was realised that Germany was rearming and had secretly developed an air force equipped with modern, high-performance aircraft, Britain looked at every possible way of mitigating the impending disaster which it knew it could not prevent: evacuation, air-raid shelters, gas masks for all, anti-aircraft gun and balloon barrages, fire watchers, early warning (including the Observer Corps and the new secret weapon, radar) and interceptor fighters with the greatest possible speed and rate of climb. What Whittle had pointed out back in 1928 was now more widely realised: there was a maximum speed beyond which it was physically impossible for a propeller-driven aircraft to go.

Maybe Whittle's engine was a possible answer? At least one person thought so where it mattered: Sir Henry Tizard, the far-sighted chairman of the Aeronautical Research Committee and Rector of Imperial College, London. Since 1935 he had chaired a special committee 'to investigate the possibilities of countering air attacks by utilising the recent progress of scientific invention'.

By 1939 Tizard was encouraging the Air Ministry's Director of Scientific Research, David Pye, who had reportedly become 'irritated by Whittle's importunity in urging that an aircraft should be built to test his engine'. Indeed, later in the year, Pye assured Whittle that 'the development of both engine and airframe would continue if war occurred'.

At a time when a huge variety of untried devices were competing for official support and financial backing, maximum resources had to be devoted to projects which were known to be cost-effective. The number of new projects which could be afforded financially, or using scarce

Early days: Gloucestershire Aircraft Company craftsmen in 1917 assembling Airco DH6 trainers for the Royal Flying Corps at the Sunningend works in Cheltenham. *(Jet Age Museum Collection)*

materials or manpower, was strictly limited, but this one, Tizard believed, showed enough promise to be worth backing.

So, at last, Whittle received the support he had been denied for so long: the official go-ahead to build an engine for flight. Power Jets began to develop what became known as the W1. It had a centrifugal compressor, like its predecessor, but with ten small combustion chambers ringing the main chamber, unlike the single combustion chamber of the U-type. Hand in hand with the development of the W1 itself, thought was now given to the best way to test the new engine in flight. Adapting an existing airframe as a flying test bed was rejected early on. The next step was to call in all projects within certain parameters from design offices across the aircraft industry to see if any looked suitable. One in particular looked promising, a highly original design by the Gloster Aircraft Company.

With one of the most evocative names in British aviation history, the Gloster Company provided the Royal Air Force with front-line fighters from the 1920s to the 1960s: Grebe and Gamecock, Gauntlet and Gladiator, Meteor and Javelin. Its origins went back to the early years of the First World War, when a Cheltenham firm of specialist high-class woodworkers and architectural craftsmen, H.H. Martyn, began producing aircraft components in 1915. As subcontractors to the Aircraft Manufacturing Company – Airco, as it was known – Martyn soon acquired a reputation for quality, and in 1917 the two companies set up the Gloucestershire Aircraft Company (GAC) as a joint venture. By the end of the war they had built more than 300 Airco DH6 trainers and Bristol F2B fighters. The five founding directors included Hugh Burroughes of Airco, who was to serve as a director of the company until it closed down almost fifty years later, and A.W. Martyn of the Cheltenham firm. Martyn later backed George Dowty when he left Gloster to set up his own business, and became the first chairman of Dowty's new company.

Aircraft production slid rapidly into the doldrums after the Armistice of 1918 and many aircraft companies went under. GAC survived on government orders for Bristol Fighters for another couple of years and the directors bravely decided to continue as planemakers, buying the business from the liquidators when Airco was closed down in 1920. They had started on a contract to build the Nighthawk fighter, a successor to one of the First World War's best and most successful fighters, the Royal Aircraft Factory's SE5A. The Nighthawk would have become Britain's front-line fighter if the war had continued. It was a superb design, let down by the disastrous ABC Dragonfly engine which had been ordered in huge numbers as the main power plant for the RAF of 1919.

The new company's first design of its own was Henry Folland's Bamel racer of 1921. Test pilot Jimmy James sits on the engine cowling while Folland himself reclines on the grass at Brockworth airfield, wearing his characteristic homburg hat, wing collar and spats. *(Jet Age Museum Collection)*

Gloucestershire Mars VI
Nighthawk fighters being
prepared for RAF trials in 1922.
(Jet Age Museum Collection)

When the contract was cancelled, GAC bought the design rights and the completed and uncompleted airframes. Re-engined versions were trialled with the RAF – its first radial-engined fighter – and were built for the Fleet Air Arm, the Royal Hellenic Air Force and in quantity for the Imperial Japanese Navy. GAC also engaged Henry Folland, the designer of the SE5A and the Nighthawk. Folland proceeded to put the fledgling company on the map with a series of racing landplanes and seaplanes derived from his fighter. The Nighthawk led to the Grebe fighter of 1923, followed by the beefier Gamecock of 1925, both ordered in quantity for the RAF.

Foreign orders were coming in, too, and in 1926 the company changed its name to Gloster Aircraft – the word 'Gloucestershire' was too much for many overseas customers to pronounce. The company was riding high, and Folland's beautiful racing seaplanes, the Gloster IV and the Golden Arrow, featured in the thrilling international Schneider Trophy contests. Production of all other types had been transferred by now to Gloster's new factory at Hucclecote and the adjoining Brockworth airfield, just east of Gloucester.

But the trend now was for all-metal construction, and Gloster soon lost out to Armstrong-Whitworth's Siskin, Bristol's Bulldog and Hawker's Fury. A succession of experimental types kept the design department busy, and the manufacture of the all-metal Siskin and steel wings for other non-Gloster aircraft kept the company solvent – just. But the 1930–31 slump followed and between 1930 and 1933 Gloster built only five aircraft – not just types, but individual aircraft – of its own design.

Director Hugh Burroughes was determined to keep the company afloat. Underutilised hangars were sublet for storing charabancs, for an indoor tennis court and even for raising pigs and growing mushrooms.

One of Folland's beautiful racing seaplanes built to compete in the international Schneider Trophy contest, the Gloster IVA of 1927. *(Jet Age Museum Collection)*

Burroughes was also deputy chairman of the industry's trade association, the Society of British Aircraft Constructors (SBAC), and was in discussion with the Air Ministry, which was taking steps at this time towards reducing the number of companies in the industry. At the same time Hawker was thriving and RAF orders were dominated by its Hart and Fury types. In May 1934 Hawker approached Gloster with a takeover proposal. It was clear to Burroughes that Hawker could provide 'a prolonged period of full employment for all GAC personnel'. The Gloster board accepted this in June and the firm's independence was over – but its workforce had survived. Burroughes continued as a director, while the able Frank McKenna was appointed production manager and later became general manager.

Soon afterwards Gloster's design fortunes were also revived when the company received a production order in 1935 for Folland's Gauntlet fighter. Its successor, the Gladiator, was ordered in even greater numbers and, as the RAF's last biplane fighter, went on to win fame in many theatres of war. The Hawker takeover was also followed by substantial extensions to the factory. Between 1935 and 1939 available floor space rose to almost 1 million square feet, largely thanks to the initiative of group managing director Frank Spencer Spriggs and his chairman, Thomas Sopwith.

After his Gladiator had first flown in 1934, Folland stayed on to design a monoplane fighter to specification F5/34 but no orders were forthcoming. It became clear that Hawker's chief designer, Sydney Camm – lacking Folland's humour and charm, but with a string of successful designs to his credit – was very much in the ascendant. Folland could not bear the lack of autonomy after the Hawker takeover, and felt that the new parent company would favour Camm's designs over his own. When his latest

Gloster personnel in 1932 standing beside the TC33 bomber-transport, the largest aircraft built by the company. Jack Johnstone, on the right, was later in charge of building the two E28/39s. *(Jet Age Museum Collection)*

Gloster's famous Gladiator, designed by Henry Folland, was the last RAF biplane fighter. This amateur snapshot shows Gladiators for the Belgian Air Force lined up in front of Gloster's Belfast hangars in late 1937 or early 1938. *(Tim Kershaw Collection)*

The hazards of production testing: the remains of Gladiator K7976 on the edge of Gloster's Brockworth airfield after it shed all four wings in flight on 24 June 1937. Pilot Maurice Summers parachuted to safety, although he suffered permanent damage to one foot. *(Jet Age Museum Collection)*

design, the F5/34 monoplane, was unsuccessful in winning orders against R.J. Mitchell's Spitfire and Camm's Hurricane, he decided to set up his own company. His track record was good enough for him to raise funds to purchase British Marine at Hamble. He left Gloster in 1937, accompanied by H.E. Preston, his trusty stressman since Royal Aircraft Factory days more than twenty years before, to set up the Folland Aircraft Company.

Folland was succeeded as chief designer by George Carter, who had been Camm's boss at Hawker in the early 1920s; their relationship seems to have been an uneasy one. Camm took over as chief designer at Hawker in September 1925 and Carter went on to Short Brothers and de Havilland before transferring to Gloster in 1931. Carter was at Gloster when it was taken over by Hawker in 1934. The following year he was transferred to Avro in Manchester, by then another member company of the Hawker Siddeley group. He returned to Gloster in December 1936. For his part, Camm wanted to close down the Gloster design office, but Carter was now back at Gloster from Avro. According to his son Peter, he told Hawker that he would resign if he was not made chief designer. He got the job.

Speaking in 1967, Hugh Burroughes said that in retrospect it seemed obvious from a national viewpoint that the Gloster board did the right thing in joining forces with Hawker 'although it led to Folland leaving us'. The rightness of the decision, he said, 'became even more apparent when only a year or so later Hawker took over Armstrong Siddeley, A.V. Roe, Armstrong Whitworth Aircraft, Armstrong Siddeley Motors, High Duty Alloys and Air Service Training. The combine was undoubtedly of greater service to the war effort than the individual units would have been.'

Typhoon production in the big Gloster assembly shop. Some Typhoon 1Bs of the company's fourth batch of 600 aircraft were converted on the production line from the 'car door' to the sliding canopy version. *(Jet Age Museum Collection)*

Indeed, between 1937 and 1945 Gloster went on to build 746 Gladiators and a staggering 6,250 Hawker types in its main factory (200 Henleys, 2,750 Hurricanes and 3,300 Typhoons), as well as the Albemarles which were built in the Shadow Factory on No. 2 Site. At the peak of production, Gloster was producing a Hurricane every four hours, day and night, as well as sending some twenty to twenty-five sets of Hurricane wings a week to the parent company, Hawker. Employment at the factory rose from fewer than 2,500 in 1937 to 7,229 in 1940 and 10,968 in September the following year.

It was in 1934, the year of the Hawker takeover, that Sid Dix joined Gloster. Speaking in 2003, at the age of eighty-four, he recalled joining the company as a fifteen-year-old 'shop boy' working with the 'chippies' (the woodworkers). His job involved getting to work half an hour before the men 'to get the glue pots going' when the animal-based glue had to be heated before use. He worked in No. 2 Hangar, an erecting shop and flight shed which was also used for wing-building, under a bowler-hatted foreman, Joe Pinions. 'Most of the chippies were Martyn's people,' he said – men who had come to Gloster from H.H. Martyn in Cheltenham, the company which had co-founded the aircraft company in 1917 – and Pinions too was 'an ex-Martyn man'.

'As a boy I was at everybody's beck and call,' Dix remembered. He moved on to helping fit gun-mounting rings to Gloster-built Hawker Hart and Audax two-seaters, working with Don Carr, who later became flight shed manager. Dix became an apprentice in 1935 and transferred to No. 1 Hangar, the fitting shop, where he spent a year or so working on detail components with Bill Drew and Norman Sarson. That and the following year also saw him working in No. 4 Hangar, the sheet metal shop, on 'a lot of rebuilds', in No. 5 (the erecting shop) and No. 6 (the fitting shop). Late in 1936 and through the next year he was in the tool room in No. 7 Hangar, which also housed the machine shop. Then, in 1938, he transferred to the experimental department in No. 3 Hangar, where two years later he was to start to build Britain's first jet.

Looking back, Dix described his time in the experimental shop as 'the happiest days of my working life'. Initially he was assigned to George Carter's F9/37 twin-engined fighter – 'I worked all hours on that' – preparing the Taurus and the Peregrine (the two versions of the F9/37, named after the engines which powered them) for test flights under the leadership of 'Chiefy' Mills, a veteran of the First World War.

One of Dix's jobs was removing the gun turret from the Taurus-engined version of the F9/37 in order to fit a second seat. This was flown by Jerry Sayer with test pilot Jack Hathorn on board to operate Taurus test equipment. Both F9/37s were subsequently used for aileron testing at Brockworth and with the Royal Aircraft Establishment (RAE). Dix was one of the 'aileron change gang' which had the task of fitting the interchangeable fabric-, aluminium- and magnesium-covered ailerons.

Also in the experimental hangar at the time of the F9/37 testing, hidden behind shuttering, was a full-size wooden mock-up of a big twin-boom fighter designed by George Carter, complete except for having stub wings, which had been built by the chippies under an ex-Martyn foreman

Carter's first design for Gloster after becoming chief designer in 1937 was the heavily-armed F9/37 high-performance fighter, seen here at Brockworth with Bristol Taurus engines. It first flew on 3 April 1939, three weeks before Frank Whittle's first visit to the Gloster factory. *(© Crown Copyright/MOD)*

It was George Carter's innovative proposal for a heavily armed fighter to specification F18/37 which first attracted Whittle to the Gloster Aircraft Company. The winning F18/37 design, by Hawker chief designer Sydney Camm, went into production in the Gloster factory as the Typhoon. *(Jet Age Museum Collection)*

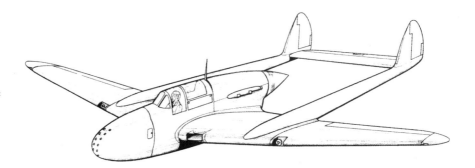

called Stait. This was Gloster's submission for Air Ministry specification F18/37 – the eighteenth specification of 1937, issued in March 1938, with the prefix F denoting fighter – for a 400mph single-seat fighter with no fewer than twelve Browning machine-guns 'capable of operating anywhere in the world . . . as a replacement for the Spitfire and Hurricane'. Dix understood that it had been designed for long-range desert warfare.

Carter's F18/37 contender differed radically from the winning design by Sydney Camm, which would go into service as the Hawker Typhoon and be built in the Gloster factory. It was an impressive project nonetheless, although it was held back by problems with its proposed Napier Sabre engine. In particular, its twin-boom configuration was one which Whittle already had in mind as a possible layout for a first jet-propelled aircraft.

It was this design of George Carter's which first attracted Whittle to Gloster when he and the Air Ministry were looking for projects which might be suitable for flight testing the new jet engine.

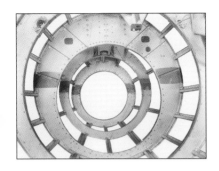

DESIGNING AND
BUILDING THE E28

'I first visited the Gloster works on 29 April 1939 with Mac Reynolds, and met Summers, Michael Daunt, Jerry Sayer and Carter,' Frank Whittle wrote. 'I had met Carter once before and had known Summers at Digby. I had also met Jerry Sayer before.' The visit had been arranged following the Air Ministry's search for suitable projects, of which Carter's F18/37 seemed the most promising. Reynolds was Wg Cdr J.H. McC. Reynolds, now the Air Ministry Overseer, the Ministry's permanent presence at Gloster. He evidently rated Carter's abilities and had arranged for Whittle and Carter to meet. A few years earlier, when Reynolds was a flying officer, he and Whittle had filed a joint patent application for using an independent engine to drive the supercharger of the main engine. Mac, as he was known, had been a colleague of Whittle's at Felixstowe, where he was the officer in charge of the engine repair section. He would later retire as a group captain. Whittle and he were both 'plumbers', Reynolds said, so they talked the same language.

Summers was a young test pilot, Maurice Summers, who was sitting in the outer office when Whittle arrived. He recalled that he and Whittle recognised each other, and that it was he who actually introduced Whittle to Carter. Summers learned to fly in 1930 and served in the RAF and Fleet Air Arm before joining Hawker in 1934, the year the company bought Gloster. He worked at Gloster between 1937 and 1940, testing Gladiators, Hurricanes and Henleys. He led the Gloster mission to China in 1937–8 which assembled thirty-six Gladiators in makeshift rattan huts on the outskirts of Canton under daily Japanese bombing. Moving on to Vickers, where his brother Mutt was senior test pilot, he then served with the British Air Commission in the USA in 1941–3 before returning to Vickers at Weybridge. He emigrated to the United States in 1947 and became a governor of the New York Stock Exchange in 1970–72 before he retired.

Carter and Whittle evidently hit it off straightaway. There was quite a disparity in ages – Carter, fifty in 1939, was eighteen years Whittle's senior – but they were clearly on the same wavelength from the start. Whittle said: 'I told them as much as they could have found out from an examination of patent records. I gave Carter some idea of the nature of the engine. It was agreed that we should try and get the Air Ministry to make official contact with the Gloster company.' Carter briefed Whittle on his F18/37 design and showed him the mock-up.

In October 1938, six months before Whittle's first visit to Gloster, three company test pilots pose with Belgian Air Force pilots before delivering a squadron of new Gladiators: Michael Daunt (third from left), Jerry Sayer (fifth from left) and Maurice Summers (ninth from left, still with a walking stick sixteen months after his crash). *(Russell Adams Collection)*

Test pilot John Grierson says that Carter himself had patented a design for a gas turbine at the age of twenty-two, while Gloster director Hugh Burroughes remarked, 'Carter was most intrigued to hear about the progress of the jet engine because he had himself worked on something of the same kind in the early 1920s.' It has not been possible to confirm this or find any evidence for the claims. Searches for patents in Carter's name around that time have drawn a blank. What we do know is that Carter finished his apprenticeship with W.H. Allen of Bedford in 1912. Allen was a major producer of marine steam turbines, including those which powered the *Titanic*. We know too that Carter continued to be involved with propulsion, as a designer of internal combustion engines and transmission units, before he entered the aircraft industry in 1916.

It is clear that Carter grasped the significance of Whittle's invention straightaway. Reynolds informed the Air Ministry that Gloster was interested, and soon afterwards research and development chief William Farren asked Carter to visit him and the director of scientific research, David Pye. Hugh Burroughes says that Carter asked if he could have a demonstration of the new engine, so a visit to Lutterworth was arranged.

Carter wrote later:

My introduction to the jet engine took place in September 1939, when asked by the Air Ministry if we would take on the job of designing a jet-propelled aeroplane. I went to renew my acquaintance with Frank Whittle and to see his jet engine at work. After some preliminary talk and a look over a few of the drawings, we went along to the test bay and I had my first sight of a gas-turbine-cum-jet-propulsion unit. It seemed to me to be a quaint sort of contraption – rather on the rough and ready side – and by no means the kind of thing to inspire confidence as a prospective power installation.

It started working with a characteristic muffled thud as the fuel mixture was ignited, and was quickly speeded up to register a modest amount of thrust, which to the best of my recollection was about 400lb. Some parts of the engine casing showed a dull red heat which, combined with an intensely high-pitched volume of noise, made it seem as though the engine might at any moment disintegrate in bits and pieces.

Reporting back to Gloster, Carter told Burroughes: 'We went to the test bed and watched a run. The intensity of the noise was just about the limit. Some part of the engine glowed a dull red colour. It seemed to me that I had never seen a more unpromising contraption to be asked to put inside an aeroplane. If, however, so much could be accomplished under the rudimentary conditions obtaining at Lutterworth, it was not difficult to foresee immense possibilities for future development.'

Another visit to Lutterworth was arranged, this time with Hawker Siddeley group directors Thomas Sopwith and Frank Spriggs, who gave the project what Hugh Burroughes called 'a helpful if cautious blessing'. Farren, Pye and Tizard were more optimistic. 'They were more closely in touch with Frank Whittle and more impressed by his dedication and by the progress of the engine,' Burroughes said. 'There is little doubt that they were also influenced by the evident willingness of Whittle and Carter to collaborate.' Tizard also realised that potentially the jet could outclass the piston engine in speed and altitude, essential attributes for defence against the next generation of German bombers.

Burroughes went on to say: 'I saw a run on the engine myself at Lutterworth and I cannot improve on George Carter's first impression. In those days one did not look at a jet engine on its test bed from the safety of a solidly built cabin and a specially reinforced glass window. We stood in the test bed shed alongside the engine and I may add as near the exit door as possible. It was a fearsome sight and the noise was a shattering roar and crackle.'

He was certainly keen for Gloster to build the airframe and also proposed to the Hawker Siddeley board that group member Armstrong Siddeley should build jet engines, but Power Jets wanted to stay independent of manufacturers of conventional aero engines, and the rest of the Hawker Siddeley board was also less than enthusiastic. There is no evidence that Hawker, as the senior company in the group, wanted to become involved in designing the jet aeroplane. It has been said that Sydney Camm was offered the opportunity to design the first jet and turned it down, as he was too busy developing the Typhoon and its successor, the Tempest. Camm certainly had a reputation at the time for designing excellent, highly successful military aircraft – even if Folland had managed to break into Camm's long run of successes with his Gladiator – and he may have been wary of taking on something novel, untried and possibly destined to be a time-wasting dead end.

Burroughes said that Gloster got the job simply because of the availability of its design staff. 'By sheer accident . . . in August 1939 the design programme at Brockworth was such that a sizeable part of the Drawing Office under W.G. Carter . . . was available to tackle the first jet-powered aircraft in this country; but for this the jet-engined aircraft might well have gone to some other firm. Some of us would naturally like to think that [Gloster] was specially selected for this job, but the plain fact is, we just happened to be available.' Richard Walker said of Carter agreeing to take on the project, 'He had to, to survive. We had nothing else to do!' This may be so, but it still seems that Whittle's preference at the time for a twin-boom design led him to Carter, who was working on just such a project. And Burroughes did concede that 'much of the success of the operation was undoubtedly due to the way George Carter and Whittle cooperated and Whittle was not always easy to handle'.

Unlike Camm, Carter had a reputation to restore, rather than to maintain. Maurice Summers later remarked that, when Whittle first met him, Carter had recently successfully dried out after a period with an alcohol problem and was keen to prove himself once more. If he could make a success of this extraordinary new technological advance, he would indeed have proved himself. Carter himself said that he 'felt convinced that the prospect of ultimately successful development of the engine far outweighed the very hazardous nature of the enterprise in accepting responsibility for putting it inside an aeroplane'.

Carter's F18/37 design did not become the new RAF fighter. Not only was Camm's design adopted, as the Typhoon, but apart from the first few prototypes, all production Typhoons – no fewer than 3,300 of them – were built in Gloster's factory. The F18/37 mock-up, Dix recalled, 'was cut up and taken away before we started on the E28'.

Carter and Whittle corresponded and, in Carter's words, the design of an experimental aircraft was soon under way. 'It was based on the then almost unexplored region of high subsonic speed and rightly regarded by the Gloster, Power Jets and Royal Aircraft Establishment teams as a very intriguing proposition,' he wrote. They rejected the twin-boom design after all, realising early on that not enough was known about the effect the jet efflux would have on the tail surfaces. Carter then proposed a highly unconventional tail-first or canard layout, but this was rejected by Power Jets as too radical, and a more conventional layout was agreed.

Carter's earliest letter about the new jet aircraft in the National Archives is dated soon afterwards, 11 October 1939, but it is clear from the content that there had been earlier correspondence. It discusses the design of the air intake, and Carter also asks if Whittle can reduce the diameter of his new jet engine across the combustion chambers by 4 inches to improve the lines of the fuselage.

Two days later, Whittle noted, there was a meeting at the RAE to discuss Gloster's proposals and arrange for any model tests required. 'At this meeting Carter produced drawings showing two possible arrangements, one with the duct extending to the rear of the tail and the other with a short duct.' Carter's original design notes were in a foolscap-size folder bearing the Gloster Aircraft Company crest and the title 'Secret and

Confidential: Gloster High Speed Aircraft'. It survives as part of the Whittle archive in the National Archives. Some eighteen months before the new aeroplane was rolled out at Brockworth in April 1941, Carter wrote:

The design of this aircraft is arranged as a mid-wing monoplane with the pilot well forward of the wing and the engine installation well aft of the main spar of the wing. Two alternative schemes are being considered; one having a normal fuselage with the propelling jet emerging behind the tail. The other scheme is for the tail surfaces to be supported by an extension boom following the lines of the pilot's head fairing, leaving the engine bay clear of all structural considerations. In this case the engine installation is suitably faired on the basis of a short exhaust pipe. This scheme has much to commend its adoption from the point of view of engine accessibility and other important considerations. Drawings of both schemes accompany these notes to form a basis for discussion and further investigation.

The design of a suitable airframe, exploiting fully the unique advantage of jet propulsion, has been considered from the point of view of first satisfying all requirements of strength and structural rigidity, together with good control and stability over the speed range. To do this necessarily implies some limitation on the theoretical optimum performance obtainable with this engine. Even so, the performance from every point of view is quite exceptional as will be seen by reference to the performance summary following these notes.

. . . It is proposed to build the main plane as a complete unit, exploiting as much as possible the use of compressed wood. . . . The fuselage is arranged in units. . . . One unit provides the cabin for the pilot. This section is proposed in timber, possibly diagonal plies on formers and stringers. The air duct passes through this unit and is proposed moulded in synthetic material. This compartment is also convenient for housing a 20mm gun installation. . . . In general the design is of great simplicity and when the arrangement has been finally considered and finalised from all points of view, the construction of the aircraft should proceed rapidly towards completion.

Whittle noted that the RAE had estimated a top speed of 470mph at 30,000ft, a take-off run to 50ft of 400 yards and a landing speed of 75mph. It was agreed that the design 'was now generally satisfactory', and the construction of two sets of wings was recommended, 'one of which would be a special high speed set'. Two sets of drawings accompany Carter's notes, both drawn by W.F. Spencer of Gloster: scheme I is shown in sketch C1980 of 30 September 1939 and scheme II in sketch C1981 of 2 October.

A series of further meetings was held, including one at Harrogate on 29 November to discuss the specification. Carter produced revised performance figures and it was agreed to call for a speed of 380mph. 'It was still undecided whether to use long or short jet,' Whittle wrote.

In due course the Air Ministry drew up a formal specification, their twenty-eighth of 1939. Given the prefix 'E' (for experimental), it was issued to Gloster on 13 February 1940.

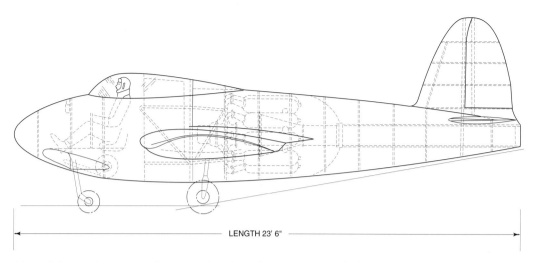

LENGTH 23' 6"

Above, below and opposite: Schemes I and II, drawn by W.F. Spencer of Gloster, accompanied George Carter's original high-speed aircraft proposals of October 1939. *(Based on drawings in the National Archives AVIA 15/3922)*

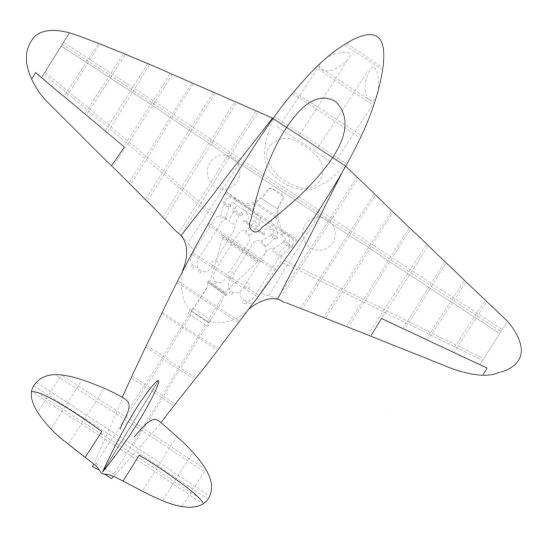

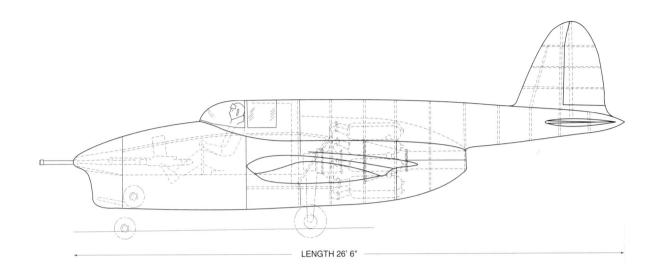

LENGTH 26' 6"

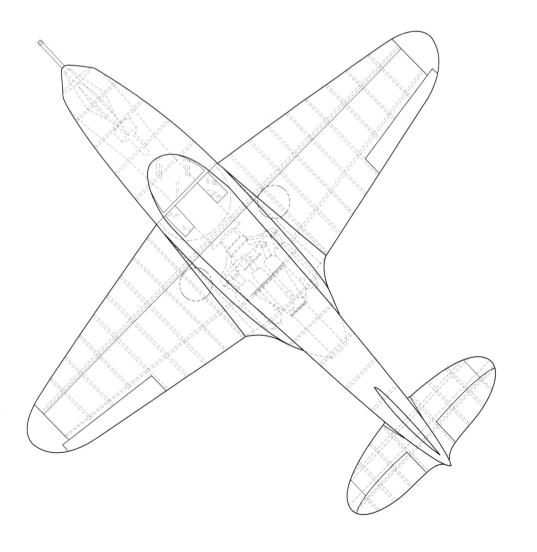

E28/39
Gloster-Whittle High Speed Aircraft
Dated 21/1/40
G40 Pioneer
File no. SB592/RDT1
Issued on 13/2/40 to Gloster

General Requirements: Operational Requirement OR77 was issued to cover the design and construction of a single-engined, single-seater aeroplane for research work in connection with the Whittle engine. The primary object of this aeroplane will be to flight test the engine installation, but the design shall be based on requirements for a fixed gun interceptor fighter as far as the limitations of size and weight imposed by the power unit permit. The armament equipment called for in the specification will not be required for initial trials but the contractor will be required to make provision in the design for the weight and space occupied by these items. The extent to which fixed parts of this equipment are incorporated in the aircraft initially will be left to the discretion of the contractor.

Operational and Design Requirements: At the maximum AUW [all-up weight] with armament and wireless equipment or equivalent weight in ballast, the performance shall be as high as possible and not be less than the following: The maximum speed at sea level shall not be less than 380mph. The rate of climb at sea level shall not be less than 4,000ft/min. When taking off from a grass surface in still air conditions, the aircraft shall be capable of crossing a 50ft screen in not more than 500 yards, and on landing, coming to rest in not more than 550 yards. The performance specified will be contingent upon the engine producing a maximum static thrust of 1,200lb.

Engine Installation: The engine [installation] shall be designed to accommodate the Whittle Jet Propulsion Engine. The installation of the engine, its controls, instruments, oil, fuel, and cooling systems and its connection to the cockpit heating system and any other ancillary equipment shall be carried out to the satisfaction of Power Jets Ltd. The total fuel tank capacity shall be 80 gallons. The fuel system shall be such that the engine will not be starved of fuel if the aeroplane is inverted for a period of 10 seconds. The engine is to be suitably protected against the ingress of solid bodies to the blower. A tachometer, oil pressure gauge or indicator, fuel pressure and contents gauge are required. A reliable method of starting the turbine on the ground and a means of re-lighting the burners in the air shall be provided. A Graviner or other approved type of fire extinguisher shall be installed.

The undercarriage wheel brake system shall be suitable for use under all Service conditions.

Armament: Four Browning machine guns, each with 500 rounds of ammunition.

When flying with military load, the structure must have an ultimate factor not less than 2 under any normal acceleration between 0 and +4g inclusive, for the full range of speed up to 500mph IAS [indicated air speed].

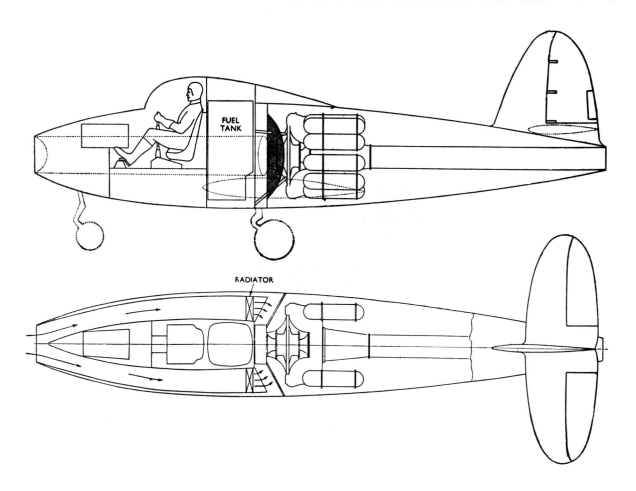

FUEL TANK

RADIATOR

Diagram of the revised layout, looking more like the final version but with detailed changes to follow.

Corrigendum No. l, dated 7 June 1940, and Issue II, dated 27 December 1940, provided for an increased military load, the deletion of armament and the addition of TR9F radio.

The serial numbers W4041 and W4046 were allocated to the two aircraft, and the contract price was agreed at £18,500 each. The Air Ministry agreed £7,000 for the second set of wings, £840 for 'test specimens' and £960 for a full-scale mock-up. The contract also included provision for Gloster to pay Power Jets £500 'in respect of the contribution made by that firm to the design of the Gloster-Whittle aircraft'.

Carter's aeroplane, then, became known as the Gloster E28/39, usually referred to as the E28 for short. Sometimes it was referred to as the Gloster-Whittle. Later it would be referred to unofficially as the Pioneer, and nicknamed by some the Squirt. It also bore the code name Weaver and appeared in recognition notes for the armed forces as Experimental Aircraft No. 137. At the time of the later Edge Hill trials, the two E28s were code-named Tourist 1 and Tourist 2.

And that was not all. Dr W.F. Hilton, who ran the High Speed [wind] Tunnel at the National Physical Laboratory, wrote in 1966:

In April 1939 Mr Lock and I visited a certain (Squadron Leader) Whittle and tried to understand and explain some of the transonic flows in his new engine; by 1940 we were working in shifts on the wings for Whittle's first test-bed aeroplane, the E28/39. The prototype was constructed by Glosters in a garage in Cheltenham Spa, and the work was so secret that it was known only by the initials GW [for Gloster Whittle]. The tunnel's crew decided among themselves that this stood for Great Western Railway, by which Mr Lock and I travelled when submitting the results of our combined efforts to Glosters.

Because the jet engine eliminated the airscrew, Hilton noted, 'the wing section had become the limiting factor on top speed'.

Although the specification called for a single-seater able to take four Browning machine-guns, it soon became clear to Carter that the W1 engine would simply not provide enough power for the extra weight, and it was agreed that no provision for armament should be made after all. As the design of the E28/39 progressed, his name appeared less frequently in the correspondence, details of the design being handled more and more by assistant chief designer Richard Walker, another ex-Hawker man, who had been in charge of developing the all-metal wing for the Hurricane. Much later, in 1948, he would succeed Carter as chief designer, only the third in Gloster's long history.

Gloster personnel were regular visitors to Power Jets and vice versa. Richard Walker was Power Jets' most frequent visitor from Gloster, usually accompanied by Ivor James and Jack Lobley, according to Whittle, although Walker himself wrote that James was not involved. On one visit he told Whittle that Gloster staff often referred to Power Jets as 'The Cherry Orchard'. Whittle asked him why. 'He explained,' Whittle wrote:

that the atmosphere at Power Jets reminded them of the play by Chekhov in which various characters would appear on the stage, say something quite irrelevant and then disappear again. . . . He said that in the first place Power Jets was quite different from any other engineering concern he had ever seen, and then went on somewhat as follows: 'a small boy comes through one door carrying a cup of tea; then you jump up, pick up a rifle and fire it through the window. Next, one of your directors appears, to ask whether he can afford to have a three-inch gas pipe put in; then the same small boy comes through another door with another cup of tea.'

Whittle went on: 'While he was still speaking one of the two doors of my office was thrown open by Cheshire, who appeared, poised, with a blotting-pad held aloft and announced "Rocking Blotters!" This was to apprise us of the fact that a "luxury" item for which he and others had been agitating had at last been supplied. This incident did nothing to diminish our Cherry Orchard reputation.' Richard Walker noted in the margin of his copy of Whittle's autobiography: 'Quite inaccurate. Nobody at Glosters had ever heard of the Cherry Orchard, let alone Chekov. The reference originated entirely from myself.'

Carter and Walker were assisted throughout by the men whom test pilot John Grierson called 'Carter's principal lieutenants', H.W.V. Steventon, Ivor

James and Jack Lobley. Information on James and Lobley has proved elusive, but we know that Herbert William Victor Steventon CEng FIMechE AFRAeS came from Oxford. After a short time in the RAF at the end of the First World War he enrolled as an engineering student at Loughborough College in 1918, gaining his diploma in 1923. His first major job was with the Steel Wing Company in London from 1924 to 1927. After the company amalgamated with Gloster, he worked for a time at Sunningend in Cheltenham, later transferring to Brockworth. He lived in Meadowvale Road in Gloucester, a hundred yards down the road from colleague Reg Ward. His daughter Janet recalled in 2003 that Jerry Sayer often visited the house, last calling a few days before his fatal accident in October 1942.

When Steventon died in 1968, his obituary in the local paper said: 'Perhaps his most notable work was that of leading the design team, under the direction of Mr W.G. Carter, which designed the aircraft to take the first jet engine in this country.' It added that he continued to direct design work and was appointed chief project designer in 1949, taking an active part in all initial design work until he retired due to ill health in 1959.

Another player in the design process was stressman John F. Cuss, later to become chief stressman for the company. A handwritten note of his survives in which he says that his office, known as the calculations

A Gloster general arrangement drawing shows the final configuration of the E28/39. *(Via Tony Buttler)*

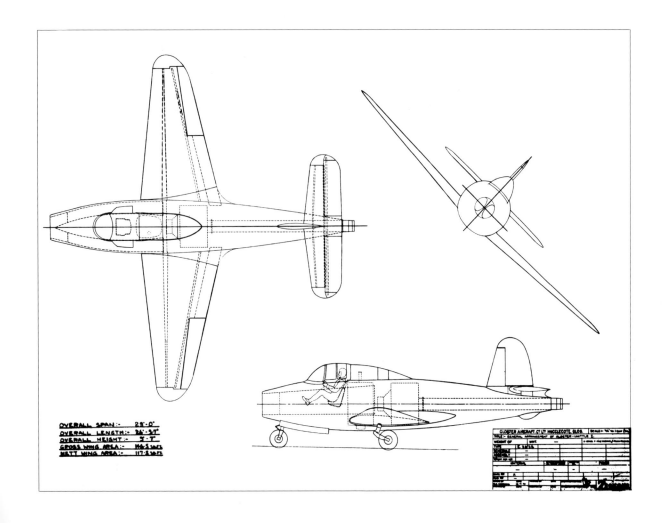

OVERALL SPAN :-   29'-0"
OVERALL LENGTH :-   26'-3¼"
OVERALL HEIGHT :-   9'-3"
GROSS WING AREA :- 146·5 SQ.FT.
NETT WING AREA :-   117·8 SQ.FT.

department, covered aerodynamics, strength and weights and performance. The staff was equipped to deal with any of the disciplines. 'One day Jack Lobley came into the office from a conference and said we were going to design an aeroplane without a propeller. We told him to take a running jump at himself because such aeroplanes did not exist. He responded by saying that it was true and it had been found that an engine which relied on a jet could give 500 pounds of thrust.'

One other man had a major influence on the design: chief test pilot Jerry Sayer, the man who would take the E28 into the air for its maiden flight. He too had come to Gloster from Hawker and had already been the first man to fly Folland's Gladiator and F5/34, as well as Carter's powerful twin-engined Gloster F9/37 as recently as 3 April 1939.

The creation of the E28, Whittle wrote, 'was a matter of continuous and close cooperation. Many weary miles were travelled between Lutterworth and Gloucester and many weary hours [were] spent at drawing boards and in workshops.'

In the end the E28/39 design was largely conventional, although since it did not need the ground clearance of a propeller-driven machine, it was fitted with the first tricycle undercarriage on a British single-seater: two main wheels and a nose wheel instead of the usual tailwheel. Maybe it was not a coincidence that the first British production aircraft to be fitted with a tricycle undercarriage, the Armstrong-Whitworth Albemarle with Lockheed landing gear, was already in production in early 1940 in the A.W. Hawkesley factory on No. 2 Site at Brockworth, just across the airfield from the main Gloster company works.

Design of the undercarriage was undertaken by another local company, Dowty. This highly successful firm had been set up by former Gloster draughtsman George Dowty with the backing of Gloster co-founder A.W. Martyn, who was chairman of Dowty from about 1936 until 1947. During the war he was living in his daughter's house near Cheltenham. His grandson John Whitaker, then a boy of ten, remembers him announcing at dinner: 'One day you'll see aeroplanes fly without propellers.' The family poured ridicule on what was plainly an absurd idea. 'Wait and see,' he replied.

Years later, Whittle wrote in a letter published in the *Daily Telegraph* on 13 March 1962: 'Once a jet engine existed, no great act of invention was required for an aeroplane to use it', although he did pay tribute to Gloster's 'very able team headed by W.G. Carter'. A more positive view of Carter's contribution was expressed in *Flight* magazine on the tenth anniversary of the E28's first flight:

It is not generally appreciated what an outstanding aircraft the Gloster E28/39 was, and how brilliantly W.G. Carter and his team solved the problems presented by this entirely new type. It was the first turbine-driven aircraft and also the first to be jet-propelled. Lacking an airscrew, there was obviously no slipstream for the control surfaces. As the jet was enclosed in the fuselage due allowance had to be made for a not inconsiderable extension of fuselage length, resulting from expansion under operating thermal conditions. It was the first British single-seater aircraft to be equipped with a tricycle undercarriage and this was the first occasion on which the single-leg undercarriage was used. The Dowty Equipment Company of Cheltenham had a hand in this. It can well be claimed to be the first pressurised British aircraft, since the after half of the fuselage served as a plenum chamber for the power unit and was therefore under about 5lb/sq in pressure when in flight. It was the first British aircraft to be equipped with an automatic observer, i.e. built-in photographic-recording apparatus with push button control. Finally, although specified for a maximum speed of 450mph it exceeded that figure by more than 50mph.

Drawings were handed over to experimental department manager Jack Johnstone in the big No. 3 Hangar, one of three brick-built aircraft hangars dating back to the First World War. Known as Belfast hangars – their distinctive curved roofs were supported by light lattice frames known as Belfast or bowstring trusses – they stood on the edge of Gloster's Brockworth airfield. The three hangars lay on a south-west/north-east axis, with No. 3 Hangar furthest from the main road, the Ermin Street which had once linked the Roman legions' settlement at Gloucester with their regional centre at Cirencester. The design office was housed in the long low building ranged along the hangar's north-west side.

Jack Johnstone had built every Gloster prototype aircraft since the Gamecock of 1925. Cyril Richardson, who worked under him, described him as a lively, pipe-smoking man from Birmingham known as 'Jolly Jack'. Dix remembers Johnstone as 'a good man, fair but firm. I wouldn't say he had great humour and he was very strict, but he was all right with me. He was called Jolly Jack because he wasn't so jolly.' His house was badly damaged in an air raid which hit Pilley railway bridge on the outskirts of Cheltenham. He was later made an MBE in recognition of his outstanding service. He retired in 1961 and died in October 1971 at the age of seventy-four.

When work on building the two E28s began in 1940, Sid Dix was involved from the start. 'I went on nights for quite a considerable time,' he recalled, with Vic Henderson ('a perfect gentleman – very dedicated') as the superintendent on nights and Bill Baldwin as the nightshift inspector. Keith Harris was the inspector on the day shift.

Dix laid out all the ribs for the wings of the E28s, marking up black-painted zinc sheet mounted on wooden frames. Although only twenty at the time, he worked closely with H.W.V. Steventon, Carter's assistant who was responsible for the wing design. 'I made little jigs so I could mass-produce my ribs. I could make one pair (port and starboard) in two days.'

Most of the initial work on both aircraft was done at Brockworth, Dix remembered. His shift worked not only at night – from 6 p.m. to 7.30 a.m. – but also all day on Sunday. Although this was in 1940, they were working initially without a blackout. Any kind of inconvenience pay for long hours and demanding conditions was 'unheard of', but even so 'I just lived for it'.

Dix and his colleagues made two sets of wings, 'a lift wing and a speed wing'. The wing spars were made by another ex-Martyn man, Percy

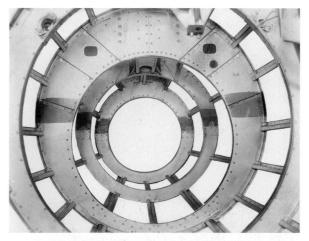

Clockwise from top left: The monocoque skeleton of W4041, the first E28, August 1940. Rear view of the monocoque skeleton showing the frames, November 1940. Close-up of the rear fuselage frames looking aft, November 1940. The engine bay of W4046 viewed from the rear, October 1940. Starboard wing skeleton assembly of W4046, without nose ribs, October 1940. Close up of W4041's fin and rudder, August 1940.
(All © Crown Copyright/MOD)

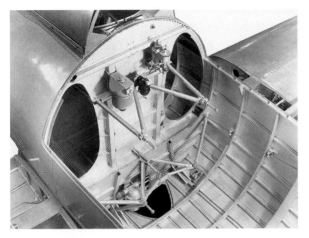

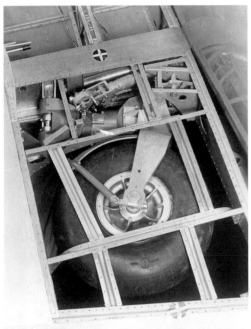

Clockwise from top left: Engine bay showing engine mounting, November 1940. Engine bay cover half open; the small square cut-out is for access to the oil tank filler cap, March 1941. Close up of the nosewheel in the retracted position, March 1941. The main undercarriage during installation, with the tyre resting on the Graviner fire extinguisher box, December 1940. The main undercarriage retracted, viewed from above with wing panels removed, December 1940. *(All © Crown Copyright/MOD)*

The tailplane, fin and rudder assembly of W4046, October 1940. Note the figure perched on the stepladder under the dust sheet on the right. (© Crown Copyright/MOD)

Gouter, who at Martyn had built Buckingham Palace gates. 'We worked as a team. It was a lovely atmosphere.'

Assembly of fuselage frames had been completed by 8 July 1940 and metal covering was proceeding. The first set of wings was coming along well. By August 1940 the first E28 had taken shape sufficiently for the first visit by an Air Ministry photographer. He was able to record the following: an underside view of the monocoque at the cockpit showing the wing leading edge pick-up; views of the monocoque skeleton; the monocoque at the nose wheel strut; the main spar centre joint; the wing-tip skeleton; the aileron operating gear; the fin and rudder skeleton; the port wing skeleton assembly in its jig; the main spar centre joint; the flap and front and rear tail fin posts; the skeleton of the tail plane; and the aileron skeleton in its jig.

Hurricane production in the great assembly shop nearby was accelerating, and the Battle of Britain was beginning. Sid Dix remembers Amy Johnson and her husband, Jim Mollison, who lived in the nearby village of Stoke Orchard, collecting Hurricanes from the flight sheds on No. 2 Site and ferrying them to their units.

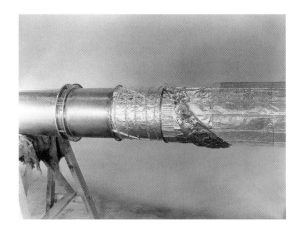

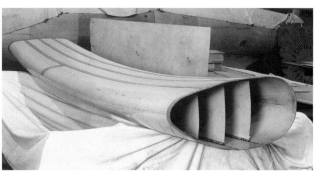

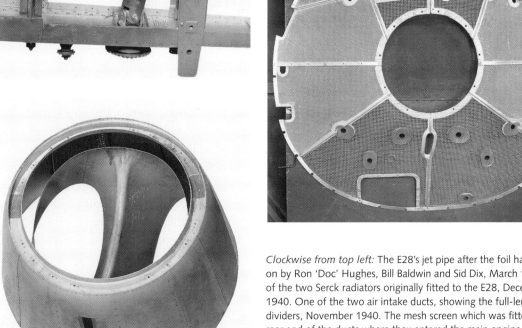

Clockwise from top left: The E28's jet pipe after the foil had been put on by Ron 'Doc' Hughes, Bill Baldwin and Sid Dix, March 1941. One of the two Serck radiators originally fitted to the E28, December 1940. One of the two air intake ducts, showing the full-length airflow dividers, November 1940. The mesh screen which was fitted at the rear end of the ducts where they entered the main engine compartment, March 1941. The nose and duct cowling, March 1941. Wing bay showing the aileron operating gear of W4046, October 1940. Frozen lubrication in this gear made the ailerons jam, causing the crash of W4046 in July 1943. *(All © Crown Copyright/MOD)*

The main fuel tank, March 1941.
(© Crown Copyright/MOD)

Looking down into the main
fuel tank bay, March 1941.
(© Crown Copyright/MOD)

The threat of air raids grew. German bombers had already hit Bristol and set fire to Parnall's aircraft factory at Yate in the south of the county. Following air raids on Supermarine, Bristol and Vickers, the Air Ministry decided at short notice in the autumn of 1940 upon a policy of dispersal, particularly for factories sited on airfields. Gloster was instructed to disperse its activities as quickly as possible, and soon had a total of forty-six sites, large and small, some of them as much as thirty miles away. All experimental work was moved off site. The design office went to Cleeve House and the Manor House in Bishop's Cleeve, just north of Cheltenham, where its personnel were installed in the houses themselves and a collection of nearby huts.

Former Gloster designer James Goulding, who later became a distinguished aviation author and illustrator, recalled: 'When I joined the company the technical offices were installed in a farm at Bishop's Cleeve, a tiny village a few miles from Cheltenham. From the outside, apart from several Nissen huts in the orchard, there was nothing unusual about the place.' Another design office staff member, John Sizer, recalled 'that freezing orchard'. There was also a drawing office in the Savoy billiard hall in Cheltenham.

The E28s were moved in great secrecy to Regent Motors, a large garage in Regent Street, Cheltenham. Regent Motors was still operating normally, with a busy workshop and yard, and the E28s were brought after dark into a partitioned-off area of the main workshop with an armed guard day and night. The actual date of the move is not clear, but Gloster veteran Joe Tedaldi – in his nineties in 2003 and as sharp as ever – said that, contrary to popular belief, most of the work on the E28 was carried out in the main factory at Brockworth. Sid Dix recalled that three or four months after construction began at Brockworth 'it was decided to rush the first fuselage. A lot of skinning was done at Brockworth' before work was transferred to Regent Motors. 'The second machine was skinned and finished at Regent.'

Chief test pilot Jerry Sayer, meanwhile, made several visits to Power Jets in Lutterworth, where he was not only able to see the new W1 engine in action but was able to handle the controls and familiarise himself with its operation.

Work on the second prototype was slowed, although we know from the twenty-five photographs which were taken in October 1940 that construction was already well advanced. The two aircraft were assembled under the watchful eye of the experimental department's foreman inspector, Bill Baldwin, who had followed every stage of its construction. His notebook survives as an extraordinary record of those times, recording drawing numbers and modifications, listing the instruments, and detailing the final checking and alignment of the major sub-assemblies.

Robert Feilden, a Cambridge engineering graduate in his early twenties, was one of the Power Jets team. He first visited Brockworth when he flew there from Bitteswell in late 1940 with his Power Jets colleague Flt Lt W.E.P. Johnson, who had a Miles light aircraft. Feilden had demonstrated the jet engine to George Carter and Dick Walker when they visited Lutterworth. Speaking in 2002, he described Walker as a 'cheerful, smiling guy', while Carter was 'rather more dour', and says of Carter, 'I don't think he gets enough credit.' Sayer visited Lutterworth 'several times', Feilden recalled. 'He was a man we all greatly appreciated. He was very much one of the family. We let him take the throttle [on the test bed].'

Finally, the E28 was ready to move back to Brockworth from Cheltenham. Les Comfort was at Regent Motors as a young storekeeper. He wrote in 1998:

> Towards the end of 1940 the family decided to move to my father's home town of Cheltenham. I worked at GAC in the shadow factory for several months. To avoid being trapped in a reserved occupation I left to take a temporary job as storekeeper with Regent Motors. I delayed joining up because of the family circumstances. . . .
>
> Regent Motors' premises were divided into three sections. The showroom was partitioned off and was occupied by GAC. The main workshop was divided in two, half being an army workshop and Regent Motors used the other half. We were engaged on Ministry work reconditioning a variety of the largest cars made in 1938–40: Austin, Morris, Wolseley, Vauxhall, etc. These were to be used as staff cars. My job was to compile the lists of components required with correct part numbers for each of the vehicles, in triplicate of course. Obviously we are now into 1941.
>
> I held a key to a small door in the bottom corner of what was then the Plough Yard, allowing access to the stores. One Sunday morning about 10 o'clock I went in to do some quiet work. When I looked out into the workshop I was surprised to see the GAC partition removed, a Queen Mary [aircraft transporter] in position and a peculiar looking aircraft fuselage being loaded. I felt like a spy and did not disclose my presence. My brother was still working at Brockworth and we learned of the taxi trials of this machine without a propeller.
>
> I have always assumed that I was the first unauthorised, unofficial person to see this secret E28/39.

THREE

IT FLIES – UNOFFICIALLY

The E28 was now back again for reassembly in Gloster's experimental department in No. 3 Hangar at Brockworth. Gloster employee Sidney Hill later wrote an account of the taxiing trials which begins by explaining the background to the W1 engine:

Work went forward to produce the first flight engine, which was known as the W1. The sense of urgency which was hanging over the whole project can be visualised. In the course of manufacture a number of components were found not to be airworthy, so it was decided to use all the bits they could muster, and an early form of the W1 was built. It was a loosely assembled version and was called W1X. This was delivered to Glosters to assist with their airframe assembly. This was in November 1940. In the meantime, a second W1X was built and tested at Power Jets, Lutterworth. This engine was scheduled to run the airframe chassis trials while the first W1 flight engine itself was tested and put through its 25 hour special category test, to clear it for flight. In late March, the E28/39 was ready for chassis trials and the W1X was installed.

Robert Feilden recalled:

Three engineers on the staff of Power Jets – R.D. van Millingen, G.W. Bone and I – had been closely involved with the building and testing of engines and their components. . . . The question arose which of us should be given the task of installing the engine for taxiing trials. I remember vividly that, as we stood in the corner of the workshop, Whittle produced some straws which he held behind his back and I was lucky enough to pick the one to install the taxiing engine. Geoffrey Bone had the job of installing the flight engine. We took our engine down from Lutterworth to Gloucester, all very secretly, in the height of the war, and I remember for the first time I had sleepless nights over my work, waking up in a cold sweat. Had we put the split pin in the centre of the turbine shaft? Of course we had, but this indicated the pressure we all felt to do the best possible job.

Sid Dix was one of the team who assembled the E28 at Brockworth and fitted the W1X engine. On 5 April, the day before the first engine-run, 'I was given the job of putting a shield on the cans [the combustion chambers]. This was a Ministry requirement at the last minute. I worked till midnight on that.' Whittle wrote: 'If the excellent liaison between Carter and his team and me and my team had been a model for others, at least two years, probably three, could have been saved. The W1X was installed in the aeroplane almost without a hitch.'

Gloster's chief inspector on the E28 project, Bill Baldwin, recorded the events of the following three days. This is an edited version of his account.

Sunday 6 April 1941. The hangar was prepared for engine runs by fitting dust sheets in the roof. All loose items were removed from the floor and the benches, the aircraft was positioned and special chocks fitted at the main undercarriage wheels. The engine cooling system was connected to an outside water supply to be pumped through the radiators by hand. During engine runs the portable mechanical starter was used, comprising an Austin Seven engine to supply power for driving a flexible drive to turn the engine.

To save money, Power Jets had bought two magneto Austin Seven engines from a Luton scrapyard, from which they built one engine and mounted it on a trolley. The flexible drive was known irreverently as the Elephant's Tool. A modern commentator, Douglas Ormrod, has remarked that it is a credit to Sir Herbert Austin's design that the Austin Seven engine was already well out of production by the time it was used to start the latest in British aviation technology. Baldwin continued:

A pump supplied fuel for engine starting. With these services connected to the aircraft and with Mr Dan Walker of Power Jets in the cockpit, the hangar doors were opened. The works fire brigade with hoses primed was standing ready for action. The Home Guard were stationed around the hangar and patrolled on the airfield. Everything was ready. All personnel had their instructions . . .

The starter motor was started, the flexible drive and fuel pipe were connected to the aircraft, water was pumped through the radiators, the starter motor put in gear and the aircraft engine began to turn. At the required revs the fuel was turned on, then the ignition was switched on and the technician standing on the aircraft wing looking through a mica window fitted in one of the combustion chambers signalled that ignition had taken place. The starter motor was put out of gear and the flexible drive and starter fuel line disconnected. The time was twenty-five minutes past six and the engine ran for ten minutes. After shut-down everyone could hear themselves again and the man on the water pump stopped pumping. With the same procedure the second run was made at twelve minutes to seven and the engine ran for eleven minutes.

Baldwin's account of the engine tests on 6 April is 'exactly as I knew it', Dix said in 2003. Flt Sgt King of Power Jets – 'a little short fellow' – did the engine runs, giving Dix the thumbs up to disengage the flexible drive of the external starter motor. Dix and Ray Lane then had the job of pumping water by hand through the two cooling radiators. The tests were

Five views of the W1X engine installed in W4041 in April 1941 by Robert Feilden of Power Jets. It was Feilden himself who painted the long strip on each side of the fuselage with groups of five lines of thermal paint to monitor the airframe temperature. Note the fabric-covered ailerons. *(© Crown Copyright/MOD)*

Chief test pilot Jerry Sayer in the cockpit, photographed by Micheal Daunt during the taxiing trials at Brockworth. The figure on the left remains unidentified.

conducted with the E28 in the hangar, its jet pipe protruding through the open doors. 'The noise was terrific. Running the engine nearly blew No. 2 Hangar doors down. A Flight Lieutenant held a piece of three-by-two [timber] behind the jet pipe – it disintegrated. There was a sea of faces watching and a lot of gold braid. I looked again and only about half a dozen were still there.'

The next day, Monday 7 April, testing and preparation continued for the first taxiing test. Bob Feilden again: 'I have vivid memories of the installation of the engine in the E28, which was completed on the afternoon of 7 April. . . . The aircraft was moved to the grass airfield, which was sodden from recent rain' (the concrete runway had yet to be built). It was Sid Dix who sat in the cockpit as his colleagues pushed. 'It wasn't as straightforward as you might think' because it involved avoiding a variety of obstacles placed on the airfield against a possible German landing, 'bayonets and all sorts of stuff'.

The E28 was taken to the far side of the airfield, where an Air Ministry photographer took four pictures of it on the grass. These were the first ever photographs of the E28 out of doors and in its completed state, although it was still in a bare-metal finish with primer on the fabric-covered rudder, ailerons and elevators. The only camera Dix remembered was that of assistant chief test pilot Michael Daunt. Facing the jet pipe, Daunt said to chief test pilot Sayer, 'Jerry, let's take a shot up its arse.'

Bill Baldwin continued:

The aircraft was pushed out on to the airfield and the engine was run by Mr Dan Walker from 1920 hrs to 1925 hrs. The aircraft was prepared for taxiing. Our chief test pilot Mr P.E.G. Sayer, wearing full flight gear, climbed into the cockpit, the engine was started at 2000 hrs, chocks away, brakes released, the engine revs were gently increased but there was no sign of forward movement of the aircraft. The engine revs were cut and Power Jets and Gloster design staff moved the aircraft manually about six feet. While only one man was pushing the aircraft it began to move under its own power.

Jerry Sayer's own report of this day's tests said:

Maximum permissible engine revolutions for first taxi trials were 13,000rpm. The wheels did not commence to rotate until 10,000rpm was reached. This may be partly due to the aerodrome surface being rather spongy. On a straight run at 13,000rpm, the acceleration was very poor. The controllability on the ground up to the maximum speed reached is very good indeed. The load on the rudder bar to steer the nose wheel is not appreciable and is considered quite satisfactory at this speed. This taxi test was then abandoned due to darkness.

The engine was shut down at 2018 and the E28 returned to its hangar.

Tuesday 8 April was the day of the second and third taxiing tests. The amount of fuel used was reduced to 50 gallons, and the throttle was adjusted to allow the engine revs to reach 15,000rpm. Before the second taxiing test Whittle took the controls himself for the first time and taxied the E28 briefly.

Sayer took over again and reached an estimated 50–60mph. He wrote that 'the elevators were ineffective and the nosewheel did not leave the ground with the elevators full up'. Gloster test pilot John Grierson said that the problem had been anticipated. It was recognised that without the slipstream from a conventional propeller the elevators might not respond sufficiently, so Carter had designed the tailplane and elevators with a much larger area than they would have had on a conventional aircraft. Another throttle adjustment was made, to give Sayer an extra 1,000rpm, and the E28 made three straight runs. Sayer wrote:

The aeroplane left the ground on each of these three runs, the actual flights being about six feet off the ground and varying in distance from 100–200 yards along the ground. The estimated run to leave the ground was about 600–700 yards, the wind speed being 3mph at the surface. It requires a large elevator angle to get the aeroplane off the ground, approximately 20–25 degrees. With this large elevator angle, the nose rises very rapidly and care is necessary not to stall the aeroplane. The length of run available was insufficient to fly for a long enough period to determine whether the rapid rise of the nose was due to elevator angle or jet effect.

The engine is very smooth indeed, and no vibration was observed in the pilot's cockpit. The throttle control, however, is too coarse, a large increase in engine revolutions being obtained with very little forward movement of the throttle lever. There is also considerable friction in the circuit. This throttle layout requires modification before the first flights take place. The engine ran very well indeed throughout the taxiing trials.

Britain's first jet aircraft had left the ground for the first time.

Bill Baldwin recorded his own version of the day's events:

The aircraft was prepared for engine runs and taxiing and taken to the bottom of the airfield. The Home Guard were positioned on the road around the airfield. The aircraft engine was started by Mr Dan Walker at 1212 hrs. Mr P.E.G. Sayer took over and made two taxiing runs up and down. On its return the aircraft was handed over to the working party. Wing Commander Whittle took over from Mr Sayer. He revved the engine up, swung the aircraft around and raced back down the airfield. He must have pulled the stick back: the nose wheel left the ground and daylight was seen between the main wheels and the ground.

The idea that Whittle himself took the E28 off the ground on that April day is appealing indeed but it is unfortunately mistaken. Baldwin maintained for many years afterwards that he had seen Whittle take off, but no other witness confirms his story. It is inconceivable that Whittle himself would

Four classic views of the first Gloster E28/39 on the grass at Brockworth airfield immediately before the taxiing trials. Note the short nose wheel leg (replaced by a long-travel one before the Cranwell flights), the fabric-covered control surfaces and the strip of thermal paint. In the head-on view, No. 3 Hangar can be seen in the distance to the right of the cockpit; to the right of the hangar a barrage balloon is tethered a few feet above the ground. On the left is the long, camouflaged main assembly shop where Gloster was working at the time on its third production batch of Hawker Hurricane fighters, turning out five new machines a day. *(© Crown Copyright/MOD)*

not have referred to it, let alone the many other witnesses. Baldwin continued:

> The aircraft went back to the working party. The Wing Commander, all smiles, left the aircraft to talk with his technicians and Gloster design staff. They then left for lunch, while I inspected the aircraft and prepared it for more taxiing. At 1500 hrs the technicians returned and Mr Dan Walker made some adjustments to the engine. He then ran the engine, starting at 1520 hrs, and handed over to Mr Sayer at 1530 hrs. The aircraft appeared to be making more noise. On Mr Sayer's last run down he made a longer hop, then handed over to the Wing Commander again. Then the aircraft went back to the working party and the engine was shut down at 1603 hrs. Mr Sayer left the cockpit and talked with the design staff. With the Wing Commander again in the cockpit, the engine was restarted at 1615 hrs. He taxied it back to the hangar and the engine was shut off at 1620 hrs.

Baldwin's account was written up from memory after the event, but in his contemporary notebook he gives a briefer and less contentious account: 'Tuesday April 8. [Engine] on 12.12 off 12.45. W/C Whittle and Mr Sayer. Mr Sayer first. Change over with W/C Whittle. Dinner. 3.20 on. Mr D Walker. Change over. Mr Sayer. 3.30 off with Mr Sayer. Last run down from road to hill airborne (long hop). W/C Whittle takes over and taxis up to Hawkesleys and to No. 3 Hangar. Engine off 16.20.'

Frank Whittle in wing commander's uniform and Dan Walker of Power Jets photographed by Gloster assistant chief test pilot Michael Daunt, probably during the taxiing trials at Brockworth.

Whittle did take the controls of the E28 and taxi it twice. A poor-quality black-and-white film of the event made by Michael Daunt has survived, showing the E28 careering across the Brockworth grass with the cockpit canopy open and Whittle wearing his RAF cap. An unattributed note in Jet Age Museum's archive reads: 'Whittle ground up packet of 20 Players at first flight Brockworth.' Daunt turned to Robert Feilden of Power Jets and said: 'Bob, thank God it flew straight.' Feilden explained why it was bound to do so.

Most historians have dismissed the Gloucester flights as 'hops'. The first flight made at RAF Cranwell on 15 May is the one in the history books. Yet 2003 was celebrated as the centenary of powered flight, when the American brothers Orville and Wilbur Wright were justly acclaimed for achieving the first man-carrying, sustained powered flight – all of 40 yards. In three more flights on that day in December 1903, the longest distance covered by the Wright Flyer was 284 yards. The site, at Kittyhawk in North Carolina, is a major aviation heritage site.

Sayer quite unambiguously referred to the so-called hops as flights, and it is clear that an event of international historical importance took place at Brockworth airfield on 8 April 1941: the dawn of Britain's jet age.

FLYING AT CRANWELL

After the historic flights of 8 April, Gloster personnel took the E28 back into the experimental shop for a detailed inspection of all structural components, including wing spars, flying controls and wheels. Then, according to Sidney Hill, 'the undercarriage legs were returned to the manufacturers. The engine, of course, was returned to Power Jets since it was not a flight engine. After a short delay, but one with much activity, the various components were returned with flight clearance papers and reassembly was begun.'

With the need for secrecy still paramount, the E28 was dismantled and sent by road to another of Gloster's dispersal sites in Cheltenham, Crabtree's Garage in Carlton Street, for what Bill Baldwin described as pre-flight testing and preparation for flight trials. It was here that the W1 flight engine was installed and a new, longer nose wheel leg fitted, giving longer travel. Proper testing of the undercarriage retraction mechanism also now took place – it had not been tested before the taxiing trials.

The W1 engine had no hydraulic pump. A hand pump in the cockpit was used before flight to charge a hydraulic accumulator up to 1,500lb/sq in. When the pilot retracted the undercarriage the accumulator did the job automatically without the need for further pumping. Sidney Hill said that this was sufficient for about four complete operations. There was also an emergency pneumatic system, which operated from a separate air cylinder charged to about 900lb/sq in, for lowering the undercarriage if the hydraulics failed. The flaps were operated directly from the hand pump.

Modifying the undercarriage at Crabtree's Garage in Cheltenham involved not just fitting the new, longer nose wheel leg but lengthening the undercarriage doors as well. Both jobs were undertaken by Sid Dix. The design mods included an unsightly blister on the doors because the new nose wheel gear was too long to retract fully into the fuselage. Dix began to make the new doors, but soon said to Henderson, 'Vic, I don't like doing this,' and proposed adjusting the uplock to enable the gear to retract completely. 'We got [George] Carter over and explained my idea and he thanked me very much.' Dix's proposal was adopted.

Testing the new undercarriage involved attaching each leg to a tray carrying weights which was dragged across the floor as the unit was retracted. Undercarriage retraction was now carried out a total of 134 times, with Dix working until between 10 p.m. and midnight. Jerry Sayer and Michael Daunt were there, as well as Richardson and Vic Henderson. Daunt went out for crates of beer at Sayer's request.

It was at Crabtree's Garage, too, that the E28 was painted for the first time, with dark green and dark earth camouflaged upper surfaces and yellow undersides. It now bore the identity W4041. The other E28, serialled W4046, was also largely complete, but with no engine available, it remained in Cheltenham while W4041 was prepared for transport to RAF Cranwell for flight testing.

Various reasons have been given for choosing Cranwell: Brockworth was small, still with only a grass runway at this date, with hills to the east and south and too near Gloucester and Cheltenham for secrecy to be maintained, while Cranwell in Lincolnshire had a long concrete runway and was in a thinly populated area surrounded by level countryside. Boscombe Down had been considered but was rejected by Jerry Sayer as 'too undulating'. Whatever the reasons, it must have given Whittle great satisfaction to be putting his engine to the ultimate test back at the college where he had conceived his novel form of propulsion.

The night before W4041 was due to head east, an air raid on Cheltenham took place while resident technical officer Bill Yardley was undertaking a final check on the undercarriage retraction. Shrapnel from anti-aircraft fire was falling on the roof of Crabtree's Garage and the electricity failed. Yardley and his assistants continued by torchlight, and passed the undercarriage as fully serviceable soon after 2 a.m. Sid Dix got back to his home in Longlevens, Gloucester, at 2.30 a.m.

Sidney Hill said that the secrecy and security of the transport arrangements were ensured by putting them in the hands of Scotland Yard. 'Two Queen Mary aircraft transporters were left at the rear of the garage and we, the flight crew, had to load our aircraft and then take the transporters outside completely sheeted up; the drivers never saw their load. RAF provost marshals controlled all movement of the aircraft from that point onward. We made an airscrew out of plywood and under the sheets over the fuselage it had the look of a fighter aircraft.'

Dix recalls the event slightly differently: 'There were two Queen Marys, a lorry and two Armstrongs with chauffeurs front and rear. There were Sandhurst officer cadets in the lorry as armed guards on the journey and at Cranwell. We took our own paraffin [the jet engine's fuel, unavailable at Cranwell] and collected the engine on the way from Power Jets at Lutterworth. We pulled up at a couple of places on the journey and people came out of their houses and gave us cups of tea.'

The journey took place on 4 May 1941. 'The night before we arrived a bomb had landed on the NAAFI at Cranwell and people were killed,' Dix remembered.

We were allocated a dispersal hangar for the E28 but when we got there, there was no room and we had to wait for them to clear the aircraft, which were Ansons or Oxfords. We were allocated a dormitory with a Warrant Officer in charge and two RAF servants. We were allowed to use the snooker room in bad weather. We had meals in the Sergeants' Mess. Jerry Sayer and Vic Henderson were in the Officers' Mess. I was 20 or 21 at the time. Bill Baldwin and Ray Lane were my drinking pals at Cranwell. Bill was maybe five years older than me and Ray was about ten years older.

When the E28 was installed in its new hangar at Cranwell it was reassembled over several days and prepared for flight. Its new paint scheme was polished and finished under the supervision of Freddie Pollard, Gloster's dope shop manager, who then returned to the company before the first flight.

Sayer arrived at Cranwell by air from Brockworth. He took W4041 out on 14 May for its first taxiing trial with its new engine and undercarriage. He reported that the modified throttle was 'a great improvement' and the undercarriage was now 'very satisfactory'. Bill Baldwin, as works inspector, again kept careful records of his own. The engine was run for 5 minutes between 2053 and 2058 hr; Sayer's taxiing trial commenced at 2110 hr and lasted 25 minutes. In 30 minutes of running the W1 engine used 23 gallons of fuel. The following day, 15 May, was set for the first flight, but the weather was not good.

John Grierson talked to many of those present to produce as full an account as possible of the event for his 1946 book *Jet Flight*. The principal players were undoubtedly Whittle, Carter and Sayer. Of Carter he wrote: 'George rightly regarded the Pioneer as his brain-child. In it he saw the embryo of a new line of aeroplanes, with far greater possibilities in height and speed than man had ever before contemplated. If this first flight came off, and he was pretty confident it would, George's aeroplane would, at one stroke, have signed the death-warrant of the conventional airscrew type, save for quite limited purposes.'

The first flight of the Gloster E28/39 at RAF Cranwell on 15 May 1941, with chief test pilot Jerry Sayer at the controls. Sayer's deputy Michael Daunt took the photograph, the only known visual record of the occasion – there was no official photographer present.

One account not available to Grierson was that of naval pilot Eric Brown, later Captain RN, who in 1998 gave a lecture on the development of jet flight:

By coincidence, on 14 May I was flying a Wildcat fighter from Donibristle on the Firth of Forth down to Croydon. I ran into very bad weather in the Yorkshire–Lincolnshire area and decided to put down at Cranwell. I thought there were an awful lot of people there and I thought there must have been a lot of transport diverted in here because a lot of them were all running around in civilian clothes. There wasn't much sign of the transports, so I began to wonder what was going on. Anyway, I went to the reception desk in the mess and was roomed up with a chap called Flight Lieutenant Geoffrey Bone [of Whittle's Power Jets team] – a nice chap but he was behaving like a conspirator out of Guy Fawkes and wasn't very talkative about what was going on. Anyway, Geoffrey and I spent one night there and the next day I was getting far more suspicious about what was going on, but he wasn't about to reveal anything. Finally the control tower asked me if I'd mind doing a weather test for them, which I did about two o'clock in the afternoon. The weather was dreadful – still only about 300 foot cloudbase – but it was beginning to lift and as the evening wore on suddenly there was this tremendous commotion and this strange aircraft was wheeled out and at around about 7.45 in the evening off it went. And of course this was the E28/39 flown by Jerry Sayer.

Sid Dix recalled, 'I strapped Jerry Sayer in. Vic [Henderson] said, take this, help him in. I handed him his writing pad. I think I was more nervous than him. Power Jets had an American shooting brake and we jumped on the running board and followed the E28 along the runway.' Bill Baldwin was precise about the details: engine started 1920 hr, take off 1940 hr, plane landed 1957 hr, engine stopped 2003 hr. Engine time 43 minutes, flying time 17 minutes, fuel used 44 gallons.

Sayer's own report on this momentous flight, compiled from John Grierson's *Jet Flight* and Jet Age Museum archives, stated:

The pilot's cockpit hood was in the full open position for the take-off and the elevator trimmer was set to give a slight forward load on the control column, as during the unsticks at Brockworth, it was felt that the nose tended to rise rather rapidly as soon as the aeroplane was in the air. The flaps were full up for the first take-off.

The engine was run up to the maximum take-off revolutions of 16,500 with the brakes held full on. The brakes were then released and the acceleration appeared quite rapid. The steerable nose wheel enabled the aeroplane to be held straight along the runway although there did not appear to be any tendency to swing, feet off the rudder bar. The aeroplane was taken off purely on the feel of the elevators and not on airspeed. After a run of approximately five hundred to six hundred yards it left the ground and, although the fore and aft

A

GLOSTER AIRCRAFT CO. LTD.

TEST FLIGHT REPORT No.: 1

PILOT   P.E.G. Sayer.

Type of Test : 1st Flight. General Experience of the type.

Date and Time of Start 15.5.41.   1940 hrs.   Duration 17 mins.

AIRCRAFT : Type and No.   E.28/39. W.4041.

Type of Undercarriage Dowty nose wheel type. All retractable.

Other Features Main wheel lever suspension type. Nose wheel strut type.

AIRSCREW : Type and No. No airscrew fitted with this method of propulsion.

Dia. :

Pitch Setting Fine   Coarse

Ground Clearance Flying Position   Tail on Ground

ENGINE : Type and No. Whittle Supercharger Type W.1.

Reduction Gear

R.P.M. O.G. Fine Pitch 16500 Take-off.   Coarse Pitch

Boost O.G.   "   "   "   "

Type of Air Intake

Radiator   Stbd radiator blanked off. Port radiator in circuit.

Other Features

WEIGHTS CARRIED : Petrol Paraffin. 50 galls.   Oil 1 gall.

Cooling Liquid   3.5 galls. water.

Total Weight 3441 lb. estimated from Tare C.G.

C.G. Position .284 A.M.C. U/C Down. .297 A.M.C. U/C Up calculated from
(Tare C.G.

Loading Sht. No. 142   Date 7.5.41.

MARKS :

Exhaust System   Nose wheel leg total travel 12" as against 10" on original

Cooling System   nose wheel leg fitted for taxying trials at Brockworth. Static

Oil System   travel 6" instead of 7" on the first leg.

Guns and Mountings   Nose wheel strut pressure reduced from 140 lbsq.in. to

Bombs and Racks   115 lbsq.in. Tyre pressure reduced from 35 lbsq.in. to

Sights   20 lbsq.in.

Nav. and Ident. Lamps   Steering on nose wheel 11° either side of the centre line

Aerial   Brakes on all three wheels.

Fairing

Type of Cockpit Heating

Pitot Position & Type

TEST INSTRUMENTS :

Ican. Altimeter No. :   Calibrated

A.S.I. Instrument No. :   "

R.P.M.   "   "   "

Boost Gauge "   "   "

Air Temp.   "   "

GLOSTER AIRCRAFT CO. LTD.

PHOTOCOPY. REF. No. P.437   Signature of Pilot

Sayer's original Test Flight Report no. 1 for the first flight at Cranwell. Under 'Airscrew type and no.' he has entered 'No airscrew fitted with this method of propulsion.' *(Russell Adams Collection)*

control was very sensitive for very small movement, the flight was continued.

The rate of climb after leaving the ground and with the under-carriage still down is slow, and the aeroplane appeared to take some time to gain speed. The undercarriage was raised at 1,000 feet after which the rate of climb and increase in climbing speed improved. The fore and aft change of trim when raising the undercarriage did not appear to be appreciable. The thrust available for take-off is 860lb at 16,500rpm and as the aircraft weight is approximately 400lb up on estimate, the take-off run of five hundred to six hundred yards is considered to be quite reasonable.

As soon as the aeroplane was on a steady climb, the engine revolutions were reduced to 16,000, which is the continuous climbing condition. The engine appeared quite smooth and the noise in the cockpit resembled a high-pitched turbine whine. The aeroplane carries slight right rudder on the climb at 200 ASI [air speed indicated] and is left wing low laterally. The port red undercarriage light stayed on when the undercarriage was locked up.

The ailerons feel responsive and quite light at 240 ASI at small angles. The elevators are very sensitive indeed and on first impressions will require some adjustment. The rudder feels reasonably light at small angles and possibly slightly overbalanced. Further investigation to be carried out during later flight.

The aeroplane feels unstable fore and aft but this may be due to the over-sensitive elevators. It is very left wing low flying at 240 ASI and carries quite a lot of right rudder. The jet pipe is slightly out of alignment, and looking up the pipe it is offset to the left which may possibly be the cause of the turning tendency to the left. Gentle turns were carried out to the left and to the right and the aeroplane behaved normally. The engine ran well and the temperatures appeared satisfactory up to the revolutions reached during this short flight.

The undercarriage was lowered at 120 ASI and the nose wheel did not lock down. The main wheels locked down satisfactorily. It was necessary to hand pump from 1,000lb/sq in on the hydraulic pressure gauge to 1,300lb/sq in before the nose wheel lock engaged safely and the green lights came on. This is considered to be very unsatisfactory. The pressure in the accumulator is to be increased or the jack is to be given more over-travel before the next flight. The flaps were lowered at 100 ASI on the hand pump.

The aeroplane was trimmed to glide at 90 ASI with the flaps fully down and the throttle slightly open for landing. The approach was carried out in very gentle gliding turns and the controllability was very good. The aeroplane was landed on the runway slightly on the main wheels first, after which the aeroplane went gently forward onto the nose wheel. The landing was straightforward and the landing run with the use of brakes was quite short.

Whittle and Carter ran to congratulate Sayer while he was still in the cockpit. Whittle said, 'Thank you, gentlemen' to the Gloster fitters, and

Sayer added, 'My part was the easy part, they had the hardest part.' No special celebration could be arranged so late in the day but the crew and other assistants held an impromptu party in the Sergeants' Mess, while the resolute Sgt Cooke of the Gloster works police abstemiously stood guard. Sid Dix remembers 'one or two secretaries acting as hostesses for the evening. Whittle didn't stay long.'

Who was present at the first Cranwell flight? Grierson names eighteen people from Gloster. In addition to George Carter and Jerry Sayer, there was general manager Frank McKenna, senior assistant test pilot Michael Daunt, Ministry of Aircraft Production overseer Wg Cdr Leslie Crocker and RTO (resident technical officer) Bill Yardley. The all-important flight crew was headed by experimental manager Jack Johnstone, his assistant Vic Drummond-Henderson and works inspector Bill Baldwin. Dix recalled that he was the youngest member of the Gloster team at Cranwell, where he was assistant to Ray Lane, 'a very very clever chap'. Everyone in the team was good, Dix said, although his fellow fitter John Godwin was less experienced than the rest. Other members of the team included Ron 'Doc' Haynes, Percy Lowe and Bill Drew. Lowe was the hydraulics expert, but Dix said 'there were no drawings for the [hydraulic pipe] runs, he did it on a cigarette packet'.

Also from Gloster were two AID (official Air Inspection Department) inspectors, Fairfield and Rickards, and Sgt Cooke was in charge of security. Rickards, who gave the clearance for the first Cranwell flight, 'was the one who got all the information for John Grierson for his book', according to Dix.

Ray Lane, incidentally, had worked for Gloster as far back as 1927, when three of Henry Folland's gleaming Gloster IV seaplanes were sent to Calshot for preliminary flying before that year's Schneider contest in Venice. Former Gloster chief inspector Basil Fielding recalled in his memoirs: 'We used to take a very small lad with us for jobs which necessitated getting inside the monocoque. This was none other than Ray Lane. . . . The reporters at Calshot made a dead set on him and christened him "Sunny Jim". One firm producing Sunny Jim cereals sent him a huge wooden box filled with cereals packed in cardboard boxes, which he in turn dished out to all and sundry on the station.' Well after the war ended Lane was still working for Gloster, in the experimental department at Moreton Valence.

Whittle's Power Jets team comprised Dr William Hawthorne, Flt Lt W.E.P. Johnson, Dan Walker, Flt Lt Geoffrey Bone, Flt Sgt King, G.B. Bozzoni, Power Jets' RTO Tobin and their AID inspector Jim Dening. The commanding officer of RAF Cranwell, Air Cdre 'Daddy' Probyn, was also present.

One source states that the following day a notice was put up in the Gloster drawing office in Bishop's Cleeve: 'Last night a short flight was successfully completed.'

Seventeen flights in all were made at Cranwell between 15 and 28 May, giving a total flying time of 10 hours and 28 minutes, all with the NACA section low-speed wing. The eleventh flight, on 21 May, was a 12-minute demonstration flight, reflecting how smoothly the tests had gone. Air Ministry official George Bulman wrote in his memoirs that those present at the *first* flight included 'the Secretary of State for Air [Sir Archibald Sinclair], [Patrick] Hennessy and Air Marshal Linnell, Geoffrey de Havilland, the two Wilkses [brothers Maurice and Spencer Wilks of Rover] and representatives from BTH [British Thomson Houston]', but it is more likely that it was this occasion on 21 May which he remembered. Sid Dix noted that Sinclair flew in, arriving in a de Havilland Flamingo, that company's first all-metal design, which was used as a VIP transport. He added: 'The six of us just got out of a little van.'

Jerry Sayer was the pilot throughout the Cranwell trials, although his assistant Michael Daunt was on hand until late on in the series. Daunt made a hand-held ciné-film of the first flight, which survives. It seems extraordinary that no official film was made, in spite of the fact that on

28 April the Air Ministry had written to the officer commanding RAF Cranwell to say: 'Even at this early stage it is known that at least thirty officials will wish to view these trials and this enquiry, therefore, is to determine the number of such visitors that can be satisfactorily accommodated at any one time.'

Works inspector Bill Baldwin timed every flight and engine run, and noted any work that was carried out. After the first flight, he recorded, the starboard radiator was blanked off for all flights and a new switch was fitted to the port undercarriage down lock. The pressure in the nose wheel leg was set at 115lb/sq in and in the nose wheel tyre at 20lb/sq in. His notes on the fortnight's flying at Cranwell are given in Appendix D.

Robert Feilden recalled:

The entire ten hours of flight trials of the first E28 prototype at Cranwell took place virtually without the engine cover being removed. The only engine inspection which was considered necessary was to remove one of the fuel injectors and insert an Introscope or Borescope to check whether any carbon formation was occurring inside the combustion chambers after they had been operating under altitude conditions – which, of course, we could not at that time check at ground level. The combustion chamber was found to be perfectly clean, and the flight trials continued on their uneventful course. I regard this achievement, with a totally new system of propulsion, a new airframe and engine, as being one of the major engineering achievements of the century.

Just one small cover was opened, the one used for the flexible drive from the Austin Seven engine which was used as an auxiliary power unit to start the W1.

The results of the first test flights were impressive, and close to Whittle's and Carter's design estimates. Carter's assistant Ivor James, responsible with Jack Lobley for the aerodynamic forecasts, particularly praised the engine's performance and said that he had never dealt with an engine before which had met its maker's claims so completely.

The drag of the airframe turned out to be lower than forecast since the adverse effect on the airflow caused by a conventional airscrew had not been fully understood. The most surprising effects of jet propulsion occurred on the ground: the heat from the jet efflux brought earthworms to the surface, and the Cranwell fire engine was kept busy putting out grass fires caused by the E28 as it taxied.

Drew was called away from Cranwell before the end of the flight tests, and Daunt returned to Brockworth early in order to make the first flight of the first Gloster-built Hawker Typhoon, R7576, on 27 May. Dix and the others remained there throughout. 'There was no clocking in or anything like that. You just had a wage that you accepted. My mother didn't know where I'd gone to and she didn't know when I was coming back.' After leaving Cranwell, Dix had a fortnight's holiday, his first break for twelve months. He never saw the E28 again.

FIVE

THE E28'S LATER FLIGHTS

W4041 was inspected and dismantled after the Cranwell flights, and on 31 May it travelled back by road from Cranwell to Crabtree's Garage in Cheltenham. Bill Baldwin noted that the water tank and both the port and starboard radiators were then removed. The high-lift wing used for the Cranwell flights was replaced by a new high-speed wing, complete with ailerons and flaps. The W1 engine was returned to Power Jets and the airframe stood idle while Power Jets built a new version, the W1A, incorporating design changes made in the light of the Cranwell test flights. No British jet aircraft would fly again for another eight and a half months.

During this time Gloster was erecting a new, purpose-built design and experimental establishment at Bentham, 2 miles east of the main factory at Brockworth. Bentham was built at the foot of Crickley Hill, right on the edge of the Cotswold scarp, in a location that would make an enemy bombing run as difficult as possible. Design of the F9/40 Meteor prototype was already under way there, and it is an indication of how seriously the Air Ministry now regarded the jet's potential that it was prepared to fund Bentham: the design and experimental staff could leave their various dispersed locations and work together at last.

Gloster designer James Goulding remembers everyone feeling 'naked and exposed' when they first moved into Bentham: the buildings were so new that they were highly visible. After a couple of weeks, though, a camouflage team arrived and with paint and nets 'transformed the big buildings into a small village set amid countryside, using the true Bentham village church alongside the Gloster unit to improve the effect'. The works water tower was concealed by building it inside a group of elm trees.

W4041 remained at Crabtree's until 14 January 1942. It was then taken to Bentham, the RAE high-speed section wing was fitted, and the first engine-runs were made with the newly installed Power Jets W1A engine. Goulding recalls the E28 coming to Bentham. The E28's engine was run 'to show everyone what it was like', with the aircraft still inside the hangar and the jet pipe 'poking out between the nearly closed hangar doors'. Several people inside the hangar were said to have fainted when the engine was run, but Goulding is unable to confirm this. He recollects, though, that 'for a long time afterwards the old E28 wing could be seen in the Bentham hangar covered in dust'.

Later in the month the aircraft was taken by road to Edge Hill airfield near the Warwickshire village of Tysoe, north-west of Banbury. This was a satellite for No. 21 Operational Training Unit at nearby Moreton-in-Marsh and was chosen because it was roughly halfway between Gloster and Power Jets.

Jerry Sayer began taxiing trials on 4 February but the starboard main undercarriage tyre burst and had to be replaced. It was not until 16 February 1942 that W4041 took to the air again, when a shock absorber collapsed on landing. Sayer flew again three days later and this time reported fluctuations in the fuel gauge. When he landed, the jet pipe extension link and the engine cone were found to be buckled. On 22 February the W1A engine was returned to Power Jets. The jet pipe was given a flexible joint and Sayer made his third and fourth flights from Edge Hill on 8 and 10 March. Both were unsatisfactory. Baldwin recorded that the 'burners and ring, flexible joint, combustion chamber, domes etc.' were returned to Power Jets. On 14 March Sayer flew again, but the engine cone buckled once more. Baldwin noted: 'Engine returned to Lutterworth. Due to the main engine cover being removed and refitted 250 worn anchor nuts have been replaced.'

Back at Edge Hill, the E28 flew twice on 24 March. On the second occasion a turbine blade failed and once again the engine was sent back to the makers. This time repairs took almost a month, but the engine was returned to Gloster on 22 April. It failed in flight again on 2 June and went back to Power Jets for two days. Sayer tried again on 6 June, and this time the engine oil supply congealed at 30,000ft. The engine flamed out but Sayer landed safely. The W1A did not fly again and went back to Power Jets the following day.

It was while the E28 was at Edge Hill that Sgt Cooke of the Gloster works police, who was in charge of security there, saved the aeroplane, its hangar and all the associated equipment by his prompt action in putting out a fire before it was able to gain a proper hold. On another occasion there, the E28's engine faded and died just before take-off. Grierson had to climb out of the cockpit and push the E28 off the runway out of the path of an incoming Wellington bomber.

At last the new, improved W1A/3 (with heat skirt) arrived and was installed on 22 September. Five days later at Edge Hill, on 27 September, Sayer made what was to be his last flight in the E28. He had to make an emergency landing after only 7 minutes when the oil pressure dropped suddenly. The port wing and aileron and the tailskid were damaged on landing.

The E28 went back to Bentham for repairs, and Sayer returned to production flight testing of the Typhoons which were rolling out of the big assembly shop at Brockworth. In October 1942 he visited 1 Squadron RAF at Acklington in Northumberland with Gloster works manager Fitz Carse. On 21 October Sayer and one of the squadron's own Typhoon pilots, Plt Off P.N. Dobie, took off to test a new type of gunsight, and were never seen again. It was believed that they collided in cloud and crashed into the sea.

At the time of his death, Sayer was the only man in Britain to have flown a jet-propelled aircraft, five months after the E28's first flight. As far as possible, he had briefed his deputy, Michael Daunt, at every stage

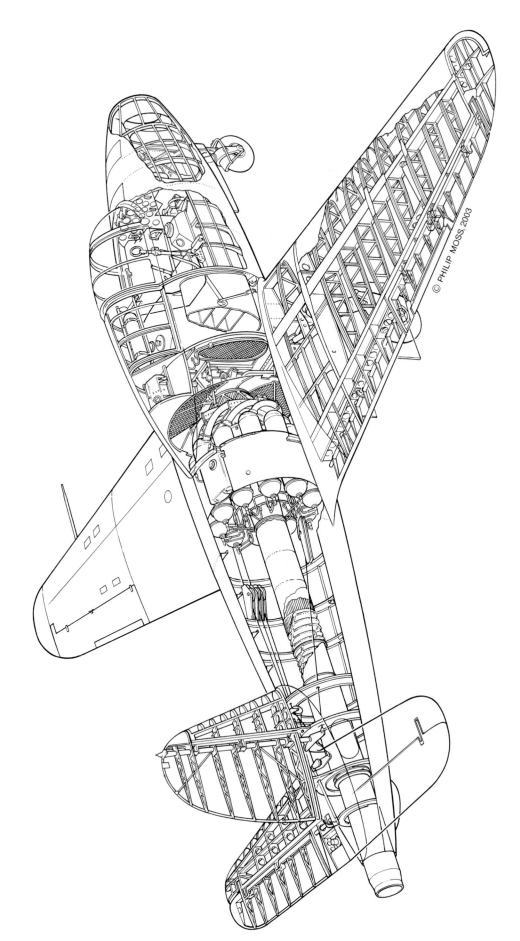

This is believed to be the first cutaway drawing of the Gloster E28/39. Made possible by the documents and photographs obtained for this book, it has been specially drawn by Philip Moss.
(© *Philip Moss 2003*)

© PHILIP MOSS, 2003

W4041 taking off at the Royal Aircraft Establishment, Farnborough, 11 December 1944. Note the finlets added to the tailplane. *(Via Roff T. Jones)*

of the E28's development, but Daunt himself had been out of action since the Folland 43/37 he was testing had broken up in mid-air back in May that year – indeed, it was while he was celebrating the return of his flying licence at a London restaurant that Daunt heard the news of Sayer's death.

Daunt now became Gloster's chief test pilot, and at Edge Hill on 6 November, only a fortnight after Sayer was killed, he flew the newly repaired E28 for the first time himself, still with the W1A/3 engine which had been installed in September. He made three more flights at Edge Hill in the next two days, including testing a new oil system.

Now it was time for W4041 to be sent to the Royal Aircraft Establishment at Farnborough, where the official body would conduct its own tests on the aeroplane. The E28 went by road direct from Edge Hill on 1 December, and on 20 December Daunt and the E28 made their first flight at Farnborough. Two days later W4041 was flown by its first non-Gloster pilot, and only the third man to fly a jet in Britain. This was Gp Capt H.J. 'Willie' Wilson, the RAE's chief test pilot. He and Daunt made seventeen flights at Farnborough in the next two months before the E28 was sent back to Bentham to have the new, more powerful Power Jets W2/500/3 engine installed.

Wilson was to fly the other E28, W4046, at Farnborough in May and June 1943, and he later flew W4041 twice more, in March and April 1944. He went on to train Meteor pilots. On 7 November 1945, commanding the RAF High Speed Flight, he set a new world air speed record of 606mph in a Gloster Meteor over Herne Bay in Kent. He served as commandant of the Empire Test Pilots' School between 1945 and

1947. Awarded the CBE in 1946, he retired from the RAF in 1948 and died in 1990.

The E28, with its new W2/500/3 engine, was transported from Bentham to Brockworth on 12 May and flew again – for the first time from its 'home' airfield – on 23 May, with Daunt at the controls. This was made possible because the E28 had a more powerful engine and Brockworth had a new concrete runway and a control tower. It was decided that Gloster should have more than one pilot who could fly the E28, so four days later test pilot John Grierson made his first jet flight, also from Brockworth.

Daunt and Grierson made seven flights in all from Brockworth, including one where Grierson attempted to take the aircraft to 40,000ft, its highest altitude yet, but he had to give up the attempt at 36,000ft when the cockpit canopy cracked. Daunt then flew the E28 to Gloster's new test airfield at Barford St John in Warwickshire, where he and Grierson continued flight testing until the end of June, when they were joined by Gloster's fourth jet pilot, John Crosby-Warren, who made his first two jet flights on 26 June. This was to be the last occasion when W4041 was flown by a Gloster pilot.

The E28 now underwent another long period without flying. It was grounded after W4046, the second E28, crashed on 30 July 1943 and stayed at Barford until 10 October, when it was sent by road to Gloster's new flight-testing airfield at Moreton Valence, 6 miles south-west of Brockworth. This was formerly Haresfield airfield, which had opened in

The Farnborough ground crew wheel W4041 out of its hangar. This is a still from a 35mm ciné-film in the Russell Adams Collection, thought to be a black and white print of M.L. Nathan's colour film.

W4041 outside its Farnborough hangar. *(Via Tony Buttler)*

An RAE test pilot, believed to be Charles McClure, in W4041 at Farnborough. The photograph was signed by Frank Whittle on 29 May 1987, three days before his eightieth birthday. *(Rolls-Royce plc)*

1939, and was where the Armstrong Whitworth Albemarles built in the Hawkesley factory at Brockworth were flight-tested. Haresfield was redeveloped and renamed Moreton Valence in 1941. By 1943 more sheds and a runway extension had been added, and Gloster was given the go-ahead to use it for assembly and flight testing. It finally closed in 1962 when the M5 motorway was extended south from the M50 junction. The carriageway follows the course of the runway.

The E28 did not fly while it was at Moreton Valence, but it went back to Farnborough, flying again on 9 March 1944. Its first pilot there was Capt Eric 'Winkle' Brown RN, the man who had flown into RAF Cranwell on the eve of the E28's first flight there almost three years before, now the RAE's chief naval test pilot.

W4041 spent almost a year at Farnborough, returning to Moreton Valence only once. During this time it was flown by seven different pilots on test or familiarisation flights. Its very last flight, also piloted by Eric Brown, was at Farnborough on 20 February 1945.

THE SECOND E28

Now that W4041 hangs proudly in the Science Museum in South Kensington – Britain's first jet aircraft – it is not always remembered that there were two such machines. Its stablemate, W4046, maintained a much lower profile throughout its career, and hardly any photographs of it have ever been published. Begun at the same time as W4041 in the experimental department in Brockworth's No. 3 Hangar and later completed at Cheltenham, W4046 did not fly for almost two years after the taxiing trials at Brockworth. It finally did so on 1 March 1943, piloted by John Grierson and powered by the W2B/110 engine. For the next two months it was based at Edge Hill. Grierson did most of the test flying there, although it was also flown by Daunt and Crosby-Warren and two visiting Rolls-Royce pilots, Shepherd and Royce. It was during this period that W4046 made the first cross-country jet flight, when Grierson flew it to Hatfield for Daunt to demonstrate it to Prime Minister Winston Churchill on 19 April before flying it back to Edge Hill the next day.

The E28 was escorted to Hatfield by two Spitfire Vb fighters from 411 Squadron RAF, based at Redhill. The squadron history website tells the story. On 17 April 1943:

> as 411 was preparing to taxi out for an operation, the Squadron Intelligence Officer jumped on the wing of Pilot Officer Doug Matheson's aircraft and advised him that he and his wingman were to proceed to Edge Hill on another tasking. On arrival at Edge Hill the two pilots were met by a Service Police Group Captain, a rare sight indeed! The Group Captain lectured the airmen on the Official Secrets Act and promised harsh results if details of their task were revealed to anyone. Their assignment was to escort an aircraft in one of the hangars to another airfield. When they arrived at the hangar, they thought that there would be a long delay, as the aircraft in question did not even have the

propeller fitted yet! But the aeroplane was ready. It was the Gloster E28/39 – one of the world's first successful jet-propelled aircraft.

411's Blue flight escorted the aircraft, W4046, flown by Gloster test pilot John Grierson, on the first British cross-country jet flight from Edge Hill to Hatfield. The purpose of the trip was to demonstrate the aircraft to British Prime Minister Winston Churchill, Sir Archibald Sinclair, the Air Minister, and other officials of the Air Staff. Matheson and his 'wingie' also escorted the jet back to Edge Hill on 20 April. During the trip back, the Gloster pilot, Michael Daunt, recorded: '. . . at 6,000 feet at approximately 14,000rpm, at which engine condition the aircraft cruised at an indicated airspeed of 260 . . . accompanied by an escort of two Spitfires who stated that this seemed to be a rather fast cruising speed for their aircraft'. On their return the two pilots were mercilessly grilled about their task by the CO and Flight Commanders, but it is not recorded whether or not anything was revealed at the time.

W4046's secret: this rear view of the fin, tailplane and parachute release gear, taken during construction in October 1940, includes a pencilled inscription on the structure at bottom right. It reads: 'The cat's revenge by Claude Balls'. (© Crown Copyright/MOD)

John Crosby-Warren then flew the machine to Farnborough on 3 May, handing it over to the RAE for the rest of its career. It made a remarkable 111 flights in all at Farnborough between 3 May and 30 July and was flown by fourteen different pilots. More than half the Farnborough flights – sixty-two of them – were made by Sqn Ldr Douglas Davie RAF, commanding officer of the RAE's turbine flight.

W4046 made more flights in its short, five-month career than W4041 did in almost four years: 134 against 110. Flying came to an abrupt end on 30 July 1943 when Davie climbed to 37,000ft and the ailerons jammed in a starboard turn. The aircraft turned on its back and the engine flamed out. Davie was unable to control it in the ensuing steep dive and prepared to bale out, but the canopy broke with a loud crack and he was flung through the part-open hood, losing his oxygen mask, flying helmet, boots and left glove. He realised he had to delay pulling the ripcord and, amazingly, while free-falling head first for about 20,000 feet, he was able to put the broken oxygen pipe in his mouth and suck oxygen until he could pull the ripcord and open his parachute.

According to one account, the E28 crashed at Lea Farm, Bramley, and Davie came to earth at Gate Farm, Chilworth, both about three miles from Guildford.

Eyewitness Derek Trice, then nineteen, heard a loud overhead explosion and saw a small white spot overhead, which turned out to be Davie's parachute. He and a special constable found Davie at what he remembers as Great Tangley Farm, Wonersh, apparently quite badly injured and at times unconscious. He told them that he had lost control and had great difficulty escaping, leaving his oxygen equipment behind. His greatest concern was that the crash site should be guarded. He was taken to hospital with shock and frostbite. Trice then found W4046 against trees in a field near Bramley and was able to lead an RAF team to the site.

The remains of the second E28, W4046, after crashing on 30 July 1943 on a test flight from Farnborough. Test pilot Douglas Davie made a remarkable high-altitude escape from the aircraft. *(Via Roff T. Jones)*

Davie returned to active flying not long afterwards, but in January 1944 he was flying the Metro-Vick F2-engined Gloster F9/40 third prototype, DG204, when the port engine disintegrated and the aircraft crashed on the sheds when overflying Farnborough. He attempted to bale out but was killed when hit by the aircraft's tail. It was after this that the Air Ministry began research into ejections from jet aircraft.

Now, in 2004, Eric Brown is the last man living of all those who flew the E28. He is also the Fleet Air Arm's most decorated pilot. From Farnborough he flew W4041 a total of eighteen times from 9 March 1944 until he was the pilot on its last flight on 20 February 1945. He wrote about flying the E28 in his 1983 classic *Wings of the Weird and Wonderful*. 'One of the most exciting aircraft I ever flew' is his verdict – and this from the man who has flown more aircraft than any other pilot in history, a world record number of 487 different basic types. 'It was a beautiful looking little craft and delightfully simple. . . . The view was superb and almost uniquely so for a single-seat aeroplane of that era.'

Only three airfields at the time carried stocks of jet fuel, and the occasional engine failure when flying from Farnborough meant landing at Blackbushe, Odiham or Lasham. 'The E28/39 was extremely simple to land "dead stick" and I got a certain relish from gliding propellerless on to an astonished RAF airfield with an aircraft bearing a large letter P (prototype) on the side, and the letter /G (guard) after the serial number, then getting out in naval uniform and asking for paraffin to refuel, well knowing there was none to be had. Always good for a laugh!'

Low pass by W4041 at Farnborough, with Eric Brown at the controls. *(Russell Adams Collection)*

It was Brown who flew W4041 on 11 December 1944 in a demonstration for the aviation press after staff at the RAE realised that practically no photographic record existed of this historic aircraft.

Brown concluded:

I can never think of this wonderful little aeroplane without thinking of the equally wonderful people I met who were associated with it – Frank Whittle of Power Jets, Gloster's chief designer George Carter, the Gloster test pilots Michael Daunt, John Crosby-Warren, John Grierson, and Group Captain 'Willie' Wilson, who headed RAE's Jet Flight. All of them were pioneers in every sense of the word, for they represented the dawn of the jet age, which changed the lives of every one of us.

METEOR AND GORMLESS

The story of Britain's first jet, the Gloster E28/39, is not complete without some reference to its immediate successor, George Carter's famous Meteor fighter. The Meteor was a landmark design and it gave Gloster a degree of autonomy within the Hawker Siddeley Group which it could not have otherwise achieved. It also allowed Carter to work on a succession of jet projects, few of which came to fruition. Indeed, only two more Gloster jet designs were to fly, the unsuccessful E1/44, or Ace – dubbed 'The Gloster Gormless' by one disgruntled test pilot, Bill Waterton – and the much more successful Javelin all-weather fighter, of which a total of 435 (including prototypes) were built between 1951 and 1960.

The Meteor story has been written about at length and in detail by many authors, so there is little to add. It is relevant, though, to say something about the early development of the project, since it over-lapped with and ran concurrently with much of the development of the E28.

In April 1940, when building the two E28s was still in the early stages, it was realised that Whittle's W1 engine would not be powerful enough for a fighter. A 'Note on the Development of Jet Propelled Aeroplanes' was able to state 'At the moment two aeroplanes of similar design, and engines of the Power Jet Mark W1 type to power them, are under construction.' However, projected weight had risen from 2,800lb to 3,300lb, so 'this aeroplane is now being regarded entirely as an experimental unit, and it will be used to demonstrate and investigate jet propulsion in flight. The problem still to be faced is the production of a military aircraft propelled by jet reaction.'

After considering the advantages and limitations of jet propulsion, authors W.G.A. Perring and A.A. Hall of the Royal Aircraft Establishment concluded that if a long range was required, the jet aircraft should be designed for very high altitude; with a pressure cabin 'a long range machine of the bombing type becomes possible'. The jet aircraft could also make an excellent interceptor 'provided the short range is accepted for fighter work. There is, however, a strong case for the development of a long range high altitude machine'.

Most importantly, the authors recognised that 'a single undeveloped W2 engine is not suitable for [interceptor fighter duties] and attention must therefore be given to the twin engine arrangement'.

Soon afterwards, W.S. Farren wrote to George Carter on 17 April:

Two shots of the third F9/40 prototype, DG204/G, outside the main shed at Gloster's Bentham experimental department in July 1943. This was the Metro-Vick F2-engined version, which first flew at Farnborough on 13 November that year. Douglas Davie, who did most of the test flying on the second E28, was killed flying DG204/G in January 1944. (© Crown Copyright/MOD)

After our discussion on 10 April I left you with the task of investigating in more detail the proposal which was put up mainly by the RAE representatives, that an aircraft with a gross weight of 8,500 to 9,000lb, with a military load of about 1,500lb, would be a better application of two W2 power units than your 11,000lb aircraft with a load of 3,000lb. . . . If, for example, you could manage to include [armament of] four 20mm (or even two 20mm) combined with a certain amount of .303, it would give us a far higher speed and operational height than any other aircraft we have in view. . . . I feel that your proposal has merits of its own and we may well ultimately decide to build both. But my present view is that the lighter should come first. . . . I should be very much obliged if you would let me have . . . a general arrangement drawing and brief estimate of performance etc., as soon as you can.

By 10 May Farren was reporting that 'Mr Carter has got out a full scheme for a twin engine fighter. . . . I instructed Mr Carter to get on straight away with the mock-up.'

Detailed design work continued through the year. On 9 January 1941 Lord Beaverbrook, head of the Ministry of Aircraft Production, told Gloster: 'I wish you to concentrate your design strength on the twin-engined Whittle fighter. This will be your main contribution to my development programme. It is of unique importance. To assist you in making this effort, work on the night fighter [presumably Carter's F18/40 derivative of his F9/37] will stop. A pressure cabin must be provided as soon as possible.'

Three days later Sir Henry Tizard was writing: 'The Gloster Aircraft Co. has been instructed to proceed at all speed with the completion of the two-engined machine, this design to take precedence over any other.' He added that 'consideration has to be given to the possible use of the experimental single engine machine [the E28] as a fighter.' He then referred to engine development, before concluding: 'remember that this is an unproved scheme. It is technically possible of achievement. The problem is to reach practical success in time to influence the war.'

Tizard then asked for the F9/40's projected performance to be compared with the Spitfire III. The report he received concluded that although the F9/40 'is estimated to be much faster than the Spitfire III at 38,000 feet its role as an interceptor would be only just as effective as the Spitfire since it has a poorer take-off and rate of climb and a service ceiling approximately the same as the Spitfire. In my view the main production MUST be on an engine giving not less than 1,600lb static thrust at sea level.'

By 19 February design work on the F9/40 was well advanced and the final mock-up conference had been held. Of the E28, it was reported that 'two prototypes are being constructed; the first should be flying in about two months and the second a little later.'

Churchill was still making every effort to bring the United States into the war, and on 28 July 1941 – still well before the Japanese attack on Pearl Harbor – three US government officials visited Gloster and met

director Frank McKenna, chief designer George Carter and chief test pilot Jerry Sayer. They examined the two E28s, 'the first of which was almost completely assembled with the exception of the engine and jet tube. This aircraft was fitted with the wing of special section designed for high speeds.' W4046 'was not in such a complete state'. The F9/40 mock-up was 'not available for examination', but Carter explained the main features of both the E28 and the F9/40 to the visitors. It was agreed that specifications and details of both types would be forwarded to the US Embassy.

On 8 June 1942 a high-level meeting at the Air Ministry discussed future jet aircraft projects, both fighters and bombers. It was decided that the F9/40 with W2B engines 'should go ahead as an operational type'. The meeting also agreed on a requirement for the 'Gloster fighter scheme known as the Ace' as a 'second string fighter'. Three jet bomber projects were looked at. The proposal from Gloster was to be powered by four W2B engines each of 1,700lb thrust, enabling it to carry a 4,000 to 4,500lb bomb load at 440mph, with a 1,350 to 1,500 mile range at 40,000ft.

An Air Ministry official visited Bentham on 16 June 1942:

I saw the first prototype [F9/40], which is very well advanced . . . we can hope to start taxiing at Newmarket during the second week in July. The second airframe is . . . ten to twelve weeks behind the first

Gloster experimental department inspectors at Bentham. In the front row, Bill Baldwin is third from the left, with chief inspector Basil Fielding in the centre. *(Jet Age Museum Collection)*

prototype. . . . The third aeroplane is being built at their Cheltenham shop . . . the fourth is barely started. . . . They have 130 men in the Experimental Shop [at Bentham] . . . and another 30 at Cheltenham. . . . the Experimental Shop foreman still complains that he needs more men – and good men.

J.H. Larrard from the Ministry visited Gloster on 24 June 1942 to discuss production capacity for the F9/40, now known as the Meteor, with Frank McKenna and Michael Daunt. McKenna wanted to use the company's dispersal unit at Stoke Orchard, but 'it was agreed that it would be very unwise to uproot the Typhoon production now firmly established in Stoke Orchard sheds', which would only be able to handle a third of projected Meteor production anyway. Brockworth was considered unsuitable, so they visited 'a satellite aerodrome at Moreton Valence. . . . After inspection this was considered to be ideally situated and the runways, with small extensions, would be quite suitable. There are no buildings, other than huts, on the aerodrome and the only aircraft there are a few trainers dispersed from Staverton.' Larrard strongly recommended facilities as close as possible to Gloster's main drawing office and factory, while McKenna pointed out the undesirability of having workmen and technical staff 'spread about the country'. At the time the E28 was at Edge Hill, which at least had the merit of being about halfway between Gloster and Power Jets, and the first four Meteors were due to go to Newmarket, far from Brockworth.

Then, on 16 October 1942, the Chief of Air Staff sent a brief note to his assistant Ralph Sorley: 'I heard the opinion expressed today, by someone who was not altogether unqualified to speak on the subject, that we are seriously wasting effort in going on with the Whittle fighter. . . . I should like to know what view the Air Staff take about the prospects of the Whittle and whether we are quite confident that the MAP are right in going on with it.' He asked if priority should be given to development and production of the Mosquito with Merlin 61 engines. Sorley replied, 'My conclusion is that the first Meteor will be disappointing, that the second will be quite good and the third a superior type, but by then surpassed by the Welkin' (a high-altitude, twin piston engine fighter designed by Edward Petter at Westland which first flew on 1 November 1942).

Another Ministry official, J.D. Breakey, reported a proposal that Meteor orders should be cut to fifty – 'The Meteor with the W2B engines will be outclassed, except possibly in speed, by the orthodox fighters.'

But by 10 February 1943 the RAE had concluded that the Meteor with W2/500 engines 'is in the same class as the Spitfire 21' and will have 'quite an appreciable advantage in speed'. It could also be in service early in 1944, while the Spitfire would be a year later.

The Ministry's H.J. Allwright, reporting on progress on the F9/40 on 1 April 1943, added an update on the E28 and on the E5/42 (a Gloster project which would lead to the E1/44 Ace). W4041, he said, was at Bentham being converted to take the W2/500 engine in about two to three weeks. 'Heat shields are being fitted to the rear fuselage and the tailplane incidence is being altered.' W4046 was at Edge Hill awaiting clearance of the Rover W2B fuel system in which a failure, so far unaccountable, had occurred. The E5/42 design 'is proceeding' but 'it is not considered that this aircraft is likely to fly before early in 1944'.

Gloster received its first order for the F9/40 on 7 February 1941. It was for twelve 'Gloster-Whittle aeroplanes' and sufficient jigs and tools to make the production of eighty aircraft a month possible. Sid Dix, back from holiday in mid-June, was employed making templates for building the jigs and tools for the Meteor wings and centre section. In August a production order for 300 aircraft was awarded. Manufacture was slow, but engine development was even slower, and in November 1942 the number of prototypes on order was reduced to six.

The F9/40 was given the name Meteor in the summer of 1942. The first aircraft to fly was the fifth prototype, serialled DG206/G, flown by Michael Daunt at Cranwell on 5 March 1943. It was powered by two de Havilland H1 engines. The order for prototype aircraft was now raised to eight, and they eventually flew with a variety of engines. The first prototype, DG202/G, first flew at Barford St John on 24 July 1943, piloted by Michael Daunt and powered by W2B/23 engines. First flights of the other seven took place between June 1943 and July 1945. The first production Meteor F1, serialled EE210/G, flew in January 1944, and deliveries to 616 Squadron at Culmhead took place between 12 July and 1 September.

The F1 and its successor the F3 saw limited service during the war but had the distinction of being the first jet aircraft in squadron service in the world. The only aircraft that was comparable was the German Messerschmitt Me 262, which was already in operational service.

A British and American line-up at Moreton Valence at the time of the Meteor–Airacomet exchange. Front row, left to right: number four is Gloster general manager Frank McKenna (in the pale suit), then AM Edwards, Frank Whittle (now Group Captain), George Carter and AM Fairley. back row, far left: Gloster's Ministry of Aircraft Production overseer, Wg Cdr R. Crocker. Immediately behind McKenna is Gloster's Resident Technical Officer, H.M. 'Bill' Yardley. Next in line are chief test pilot Michael Daunt, test pilot John Crosby-Warren and Mr Hall. On the right, second from the end behind the officer carrying a raincoat, is Gloster Works Manager R.V. Atkinson. (Ray Williams via Tony Buttler)

Gloster E1/44 TX145, known as the Ace or 'Gormless', in a photograph signed for Bill Baldwin by seven of his colleagues on the project, including E28 veterans Steventon, Lobley and Johnstone. *(Jet Age Museum Collection)*

The Me 262 was the superior aircraft and was significantly faster, but its Junkers Jumo engines had a disastrously short service life of only 25 hours, and the cost in lives of developing the Me 262 had been horrendous.

George Carter's and Willi Messerschmitt's jet fighters never met in jet-to-jet combat, but were used in a variety of other roles. The Meteor's speciality was its ability to intercept and shoot down the V1 flying bombs, popularly known as Doodlebugs, which the Germans were launching against London.

The Meteor had its shortcomings, but was nonetheless a remarkably successful aircraft and is the design above all for which George Carter will be remembered. It broke the world absolute air speed record in 1945 and 1946 and remained in production until 1955. Almost 3,900 were built, including 330 overseas, and it served with eleven overseas air forces as well as the RAF. At the time of writing in 2004, sixty-one years after the first F9/40 first flew, there are, unbelievably, three Meteors still at work. One is a target drone operating from Llanbedr in Wales for weapons testing and the other two – one recently refurbished – are still flying from the Martin-Baker airfield at Chalgrove on ejection seat trials.

The E1/44 development of the E5/42 project referred to above failed to match the success of the Meteor. It was in effect a fighter development of the E28, made possible by the development of jet engines which were at last powerful enough for a single-engined machine. There were so many changes and delays in its development that it did not fly until March 1948. Only two were built before the project was abandoned.

SEVEN

THE DESIGNERS

T his is not just a story of inventions and machines. It is also about the people behind them, and this and the following chapter pay tribute to the most significant players in the Gloster team, the designers and the pilots.

GEORGE CARTER

The outstanding figure is George Carter, Gloster's chief designer, who designed the E28/39 and followed it up with the Meteor, the Allies' first jet fighter and the world's first jet in squadron service. Former Gloster designer James Goulding recognised him in his book *Interceptor* as Britain's first fighter designer to be fully committed to jet propulsion when others saw Whittle's invention as 'a possible passing fad or scientific experiment'. Carter told Goulding in 1943 that in time to come 'all classes' of aircraft would be jet-propelled, with only light aircraft still using piston engines. Goulding wrote that this prophecy seemed 'rather far-fetched' at the time.

Carter's design for the Meteor was well advanced before the E28 even flew. It had its shortcomings but it was remarkably successful and proved capable of long development as fighter, night fighter and trainer.

Whittle's achievement as the inventor and developer of the jet engine has overshadowed that of the man who designed the airframe which first took Whittle's invention into the skies. It has been suggested that any of a number of designers could have come up with something suitable, but Carter's achievement was greater than that. The recognition he has received has been modest, in keeping with his character.

Carter's career has not been properly recorded and has proved quite elusive to piece together. No one seems to have attempted any kind of thorough biographical treatment, although his niece Sylvia made detailed notes which were later lost in Hurricane Gilbert in Jamaica in 1988. There is certainly no single, authoritative source and there are plenty of inconsistencies in what has been published. Even his own *Who's Who* entries raise a few question marks. There is not enough information for a full-scale book, but it has been possible to collate enough material to do him some justice at last. What follows is believed to be the first attempt at any proper biographical treatment of a neglected figure, the man who designed Britain's first jet aircraft. His honours were few and his fame is slight. He deserves more.

Carter was as modest and retiring as Whittle was forceful, and his place as one of the leading jet pioneers is little known or appreciated. He was very much the senior partner in terms of age – when the E28 first flew he was fifty-two, while Whittle was only thirty-three.

He died in 1969, just short of his eightieth birthday, having designed a string of innovative aircraft, not just for Gloster but for Sopwith, Hawker, Shorts, de Havilland and Avro too. His Horsley bomber almost set a new long-distance record in 1927, setting off for India on 20 May. Here, too, Carter's work was eclipsed by a more famous figure, for this was the very day that Charles Lindbergh set off from Long Island to Paris, beating the Horsley's effort by a mere 190 miles. Lindbergh visited London soon after his record-breaking flight and on 2 June returned to Paris in a Carter-designed Woodcock fighter, J8295, on loan from 17 Squadron RAF.

Wilfred George Carter was born in Bedford on 9 March 1889. His father, George Alfred Carter, was a journeyman carpenter – he later became a builder – who had married Bertha Ellen Odell at St Cuthbert's, Bedford, the previous May. They lived half a mile east of the High Street, in Howbury Street off Castle Road. Grandmother Isabella Odell, who lived in the next street, was there at his birth.

Twelve years later young George, together with his parents and his nine-year-old sister, Gladys, were living with his cabinetmaker grand-father Thomas O'Dell (sic) at 101 Tavistock Street, the main road out of Bedford running north-west from the High Street. Thomas was sixty-two, working at home, employing his two live-in sons Ernest and Edwin, while his daughters Edith and Margaret were drapers' assistants.

Bedford had grown fast in the nineteenth century, largely thanks to the attractions of the Harpur Trust schools. George was educated at Bedford School, one of several owned by the Trust, which had and still has a high reputation. Other pupils included George Bulman, who went on to a long and distinguished career with the Air Ministry, responsible for engine development from 1928 to 1944, and future Boulton and Paul chief designer John D. North, both three years Carter's junior. Bulman remembered Bedford as 'a quiet little town, well-known for its excellent schools. . . . It was populated largely by retired naval, military and Indian civil servants, all fairly poor, and attracted by the cheapness of its education.'

Leaving in 1906, at the age of seventeen, Carter was apprenticed to the local firm of W.H. Allen at Queens Engineering Works. Allens had arrived in Bedford only twelve years before, when William Henry Allen in 1894 established the works at Ford End Road, between the station and the river, setting up as manufacturers of diesel engines. The firm was only Bedford's second major employer after the Howard Brothers' Britannia Works in 1859.

George Carter was there for the start of turbine production in 1908. These were used on the great liners of the early twentieth century, including the *Titanic*. In 1912, aged twenty-two or twenty-three, he changed jobs and worked on the design of internal combustion engines and transmission units for a Bedford firm. This was the time when John Grierson suggests, tantalisingly, that Carter took out a patent for a gas turbine, but the evidence is elusive. Grierson maintains that this was one of the factors that contributed to Carter's excellent professional relationship with Frank Whittle. Sometime during the next four years Carter developed a close relationship with Hilda Back, some six years younger than him, the daughter of a South African mining engineer. She lived in Tennyson Road, only a few streets away from where George had grown up.

From August 1914 Britain was at war with Germany. After a slow start, war production was rising rapidly. One of the fastest-growing sectors was the aircraft industry, and it was here that George Carter was now to embark on the career which would make his name. Did he respond to an advertisement in *The Aeroplane* magazine in December 1915? It read: 'WANTED. First class engineer's draughtsman; must have had charge of fair size drawing office; good organiser essential. No person engaged on Government work need apply. Write, stating age, particulars of experience, and salary required, to the Sopwith Aviation Co Ltd, Kingston-on-Thames.' Whether or not in reply to this advertisement, he certainly applied to join Sopwith and was accepted.

George Carter as a young man, before the First World War, during his time with W.H. Allen or soon afterwards.
(Peter Carter)

Sopwith Aviation was fast becoming one of Britain's largest aircraft companies. The 1½ Strutter, Pup and Triplane were entering production, and the company was buying up and demolishing adjoining properties to expand its premises. Orders were such that buildings were in use before completion and women were being taken on as welders.

Carter now had the offer of a job away from home and Hilda had come of age. They married at St Martin's, Bedford, on 20 April 1916, a few weeks after Carter's twenty-seventh birthday. He was still living at his grandfather's in Tavistock Street and described himself on his marriage certificate as 'engineer'. He now joined the Sopwith Aviation Company Ltd, where he was to become chief draughtsman.

The design process at Sopwith at the time was a largely informal business conducted by general manager Thomas Sopwith, his right-hand man Fred Sigrist – trained engineer and master welder – and chief test pilot Harry Hawker, who between them were responsible for the brilliant Camel fighter. Chief designer Herbert Smith had the job of working out the detailed design from the concept developed by the other three. A later Sopwith fighter, the Dolphin – the world's first multi-gun single-seat fighter in service – was designed and developed by Smith himself. Smith had joined Sopwith in 1914 and now headed a drawing office of some fifty people. His chief draughtsman, R.J. Ashfield, was a former schoolteacher who had joined the company in 1912, earning £3 a week. Carter took over from Ashfield and was in charge of preparing the production drawings of all the later Sopwith wartime aircraft.

SOPWITH AVIATION AND ENGINEERING Cº LIMITED. KINGSTON - ON - THAMES.		
DRAWN BY	APPROVED BY W.G. CARTER	**D.3077.**
RETRACED BY G. GOATER	ISSUED 3·6·19	

Carter, as Sopwith's chief draughtsman, approved the company drawings of the civilian Dove two-seater version of the wartime Pup fighter in 1919.

George and Hilda's son, Peter, was born in 1917, and at some stage in the next two years Carter made the transition from draughtsman to designer. This seems to have been in 1919, after the war had ended. He is known in June 1919 to have approved the design of a peacetime two-seater sporting version of the wartime Pup fighter, known as the Dove. Ten of these were built and one of them is still flying with the Shuttleworth Collection, although reconverted to original Pup standard.

Carter's name was also associated with the Sopwith Grasshopper tourer and dual-control trainer, and with the three-seater Antelope commercial biplane.

His only properly accredited Sopwith design was a racing seaplane built for the first postwar Schneider Trophy contest, held at Bournemouth in 1919. It was known simply as the Sopwith Schneider, but was a completely different design from the Tabloid-based aircraft of the same name which had won the contest in 1914.

The new Schneider was a specialised racing machine, intended to be flown by Harry Hawker. Although designed principally by Carter, it was largely derived from the Dragonfly-powered Snapper fighter of 1918. Work began in the summer for the race in September. It was designated Sopwith Model 107 and registered G-EAKI. Its outstanding feature was the engine, the first of Roy Fedden's 450hp Cosmos Jupiter radials and precursor of the outstandingly successful Bristol Jupiter which would power so many interwar aircraft in Britain and abroad.

Carter's Schneider was the fastest entry, but the race was called off because of fog and then Harry Hawker ruined the Schneider's pontoons when he beached it. It was rebuilt with a wheeled undercarriage, renamed Rainbow and entered in the Aerial Derby of 1920, now with an ABC Dragonfly radial engine and cut-down wings. Although disqualified for not crossing the proper finishing line, its only serious rival was Henry Folland's Nieuport Goshawk racer, derived from his Nighthawk which was to have been the RAF's front-line fighter in 1919 if the war had continued. It was also in 1920 that Carter received his first public honour, when he was made an MBE.

Sopwith's fortunes nosedived after the war. Government orders dried up and the company faced a hefty bill for excess profits tax. Thomas Sopwith wound up the company on 11 September 1920 – paying his creditors in full – and the employees were given notice.

Chief designer Herbert Smith set off for Japan the following February, where he was to design Japan's first indigenous shipboard fighter, the 1MF1, and its first torpedo bomber, the B1M, for Mitsubishi. The fighter replaced the Imperial Japanese Navy's Gloucestershire Sparrowhawks, another development by Henry Folland of his Nighthawk design. Smith's work in Japan is a fascinating step on the road to Pearl Harbor, but not a story to be told here.

Sopwith, Sigrist and Hawker soon set up a new venture, the H.G. Hawker Engineering Company, but Carter let his house to Hawker chief draughtsman L.E. Metcalfe, left the industry and headed back to Bedford, where he found work as an engineer. Then, on 12 July 1921, came the news that the legendary Harry Hawker was dead. He had been suffering from a painful, restricting tuberculous disease of the spine for more than a year. Now, when he was flying Folland's blue-and-yellow checkerboard Goshawk racer for the first time on a practice flight, a petrol leak caused it to catch fire in the air. Hawker suffered a spinal haemorrhage and severe burns, crashing a mile west of Hendon aerodrome.

The new Hawker company kept its co-founder's name and engaged Capt Bertram Thompson as chief designer. He took on the unfinished Humpback fleet spotter design left behind by Smith and Carter. This awkward, lumbering aeroplane was the first Hawker design, but was soon abandoned, as was Thompson's next effort, the unstable Duiker parasol monoplane, the first Hawker design to be built.

Thompson next designed the Woodcock fighter to Air Ministry specification 25/22, but this too had many shortcomings. He resigned in 1923, transferring to Saunders. Metcalfe tipped off Carter, and he now returned to the industry as Hawker's new chief designer. Aviation historian Harald Penrose wrote: 'Carter seemed the obvious successor, for his years of experience of Sopwith and Sigrist design policy would be invaluable in giving time-continuity for their efforts to break into the peacetime aircraft industry with military designs.'

Carter's little Rainbow racer reappeared in 1923, again with a Jupiter engine, to compete in the Aerial Derby. Now known as the Sopwith Hawker – the only occasion when the two illustrious names were linked – it was faster than ever, but finished second. It was written off in a forced landing near Brooklands in September.

Carter's first job with Hawker was to sort out the Woodcock design, which he did well enough to win the company its first production order – indeed, it was the first new British fighter to go into production after the war. Sixty-two Woodcock IIs were built, serving with 3 and 17 Squadrons

Carter's first design was the Sopwith Schneider racing seaplane G–EAKI of 1919. Finished in mid-blue and white, it was powered by the first of Roy Fedden's Cosmos Jupiter radial engines. *(A.J. Jackson Collection)*

RAF as a day and night fighter. Carter went on to design the Hawker Horsley bomber to Air Ministry specification 26/23. It had been specified as a metal aeroplane, but Hawker was allowed to produce a wooden prototype as a time-saving measure. It was named after Horsley Towers, Thomas Sopwith's home nearby, and Carter's son, Peter, remembers his parents going to lavish parties there.

Carter now took on as his deputy a thirty-year-old, hard-swearing designer called Sydney Camm, four years his junior, who joined Hawker from G.H. Handasyde in 1923. Camm was to become one of Britain's most renowned aircraft designers, with a string of famous aircraft – including the Hart, Fury, Hurricane, Typhoon and Hunter – to his credit. The Horsley, too, is sometimes referred to as Camm's design, but it was almost certainly Carter's work. Camm took over its later development.

Carter was also working on an enlarged Woodcock development, the three-seater Hedgehog naval reconnaissance aircraft. Aviation historian Harald Penrose wrote that people who worked at Hawker at the time remembered Carter in his glass cubicle office on a raised platform in the middle of the drawing office. They also recalled him being asked by Fred Sigrist to transfer one of his staff to work on reducing the handicap of Sigrist's yacht. Penrose wrote that Sigrist by now was no longer involved in design 'except to criticise'.

With wheels instead of pontoons and re-engined with an ABC Dragonfly, Carter's racer was renamed the Rainbow for the 1920 Aerial Derby. *(A.J. Jackson Collection)*

Camm, according to Penrose, worked under Carter to begin with but 'was soon given a free hand'. Carter gave him the drawings of the 1914 Sopwith Tabloid and told him to design an up-to-date version with half the weight and power. This was to become Camm's first accredited design, the Hawker Cygnet ultra-light single-seater, built for the light aeroplane competition held at Lympne in 1924.

Following his success with the Cygnet, which in spite of its small size was remarkably similar in layout to the much bigger Horsley, Camm went on to design the Heron fighter, Hawker's first metal-framed design, under Carter's leadership. Meanwhile, Carter himself was now concentrating on the Condor-engined Hornbill experimental fighter to specification 7/24. It was Hawker's first fighter with an inline engine and can be seen as the forerunner of Camm's elegant Fury which epitomised RAF biplane fighters of the 1930s. Long thought of as Camm's work, the Hornbill is now recognised as part of the Carter era. It was not until the Hornbill returned from Martlesham that Camm made extensive modifications to the design. Aviation historian Francis K. Mason, in the introduction to the revised 1991 edition of his standard work on Hawker aircraft, remarks that this recognition 'throws an entirely new light on Carter's ability to match, and indeed surpass by a considerable margin, the performance of the Fairey Fox light bomber' – the Hornbill attaining almost 200mph against the Fox's 150mph, itself a remarkable advance on the day bombers of the time.

It was in 1925, the year that the Hornbill first flew, that Carter left Hawker. He told Harald Penrose:

There was a difference of opinion between Sigrist and myself over organisation of the technical division and design procedure. A hitherto pleasant relationship became impaired. Quite likely I was at fault, for I was inclined to be impatient. We had just been told that the Horsley day bomber would be accepted for production by the RAF. I had fulfilled my aspiration and justified my appointment as the firm's designer. I decided it would be good to seek fresh pastures, and never had regret in so doing. On the contrary it has always given me a curious sense of satisfaction to find I had sufficient guts to take a chance and seek adventure.

Clearly Carter and Camm had both given much thought to monoplane designs. Camm schemed a forward-looking monoplane fighter in 1925, with a Jupiter engine and cantilever wing. Camm's design was not built, but Carter's next two designs were both to be monoplanes at a time when the biplane was still supreme.

Carter was now approached by Roy Fedden, whose Cosmos Jupiter had powered Carter's Sopwith Schneider of 1919. For high-performance aero engines, 1926 was a transitional year: Napier's mighty Lion had reached its maximum development, while Rolls-Royce had yet to develop a racing engine. Although it was accepted that a radial engine would be unlikely to outperform an in-line one, Fedden was keen to showcase his new 860hp Mercury radial. Carter wrote:

Carter's Hawker Horsley bomber first flew in 1925; 123 were built, including 3 prototypes, 6 for the Royal Hellenic Naval Air Service and 2 Dantorp versions for Denmark. J8607, shown here, left RAF Cranwell on 20 May 1927 in an attempt to fly non-stop to India with Flt Lts Carr and Gillman of the RAF's Long Range Flight. Although forced down in the Persian Gulf the following day, they set a new record of 3,419 miles, which was broken later the same day when Charles Lindbergh landed in Paris after his epic 3,610-mile solo flight from New York. *(Tony Buttler Collection)*

After leaving Hawker I would have preferred a short holiday, but Roy Fedden proposed I should prepare this design for the Schneider contest and he would build a special engine. I was nominally working for [consulting engineer] Colonel Bristow, who had independent means, and the project was backed by Oswald Short. I schemed a low-wing semi-cantilever monoplane with wings braced by V-struts from mid-span to the float undercarriage, and a model was tested in the 14ft NPL [National Physical Laboratory] wind tunnel. We submitted the design to the Air Ministry who eventually issued a contract to build it.

Air Ministry official George Bulman, who later became director of engine development and production, wrote that the purpose of the Crusader was to investigate under extreme conditions the disparity, if any, between aircraft fitted with water-cooled and air-cooled engines, the two types involved representing the latest in development. Wind-tunnel testing showed the pressing need to reduce the design's air resistance, which was the inevitable penalty of a radial-engined design. Carter fitted helmets on the engine's cylinder heads, much as he had done earlier with a version of his Woodcock fighter, and opted for wire bracing in place of the struts.

And so the Crusader took shape, having been tendered in early 1926 and defined by specification 7/26. Detail design and construction were

Ancestor of the Fury: Carter's one-off Hornbill fighter, which first flew in the summer of 1925, is seen here at Martlesham on 16 November 1926 during its service assessment. By this date Carter had left Hawker and his design had been extensively modified by Sydney Camm. (Via Tony Buttler)

undertaken by Short Brothers of Rochester. Its wings and wooden monocoque rear fuselage were skinned in mahogany. Painted gloss white with blue trim, it was launched on 18 April 1927, first flown at Felixstowe on 4 May, and after eventful testing shipped to Venice in August. R.J. Mitchell's Supermarine S5 and Henry Folland's Gloster IVa, both with in-line engines, proved to be faster, so the Crusader was to be used as a training machine. Its brief career ended suddenly on 11 September when Flg Off H.M. Schofield crashed into Venice Lagoon at 150mph – the aileron cables had been crossed when the Crusader was assembled. Schofield was concussed but uninjured; the aeroplane's wreckage was not recovered for a week.

Carter was now out of work and for about six months he moved back to Bedford, where he worked for Robertsons, an engineering company. He came back into the aviation industry when he found work with the de Havilland Company at Stag Lane in north London. He moved to Thames Ditton and was taken on as a specialist designer for the company's DH77 interceptor, another high-performance monoplane with a new engine. It was intended to compete to specification F20/27 along with monoplanes from Westland and Vickers, as well as biplanes from Armstrong Whitworth, Bristol, Fairey, Gloster, Hawker, Saro and Westland.

Once again Carter was working closely with the engine designer, this time Maj F.B. Halford, who had developed an engine with a novel twin-crankshaft H-16 configuration giving a very low frontal area. This was known initially as the Napier H and later as the Rapier I. The combination of the engine and Carter's exceptionally neat design gave it an impressive performance. Although Camm's Hornet biplane with its Rolls-Royce in-line engine won the competition and went into production as the famous Fury fighter, Carter's DH77 performed almost as well on 60 per cent of the power.

The interceptor first flew on 11 July 1929 and went to Martlesham for testing in December. It was in the following year that de Havilland gave up its military work to concentrate on its highly successful civilian designs, and the Air Ministry arranged for de Havilland's military designs to be transferred to the Gloster Aircraft Company for further development. The transfer involved three designs, the DH67, DH72 and DH77, and Carter was put in charge. He moved to a house between Witcombe and the Cross Hands public house on the road between Brockworth and Birdlip.

The DH67 was a proposal for a twin-engined survey biplane. This was redesigned at Gloster under chief designer Henry Folland's leadership as the Gloster AS31.

In June 1930 Carter's DH77 interceptor took part in the annual RAF display at Hendon, where Penrose described it as the 'only . . . notable aerodynamic military advance of that year'. In September it went to Gloster at Brockworth for a 100-hour test and was handed over for development. It then went for its Martlesham trials in December, spent two more years at Brockworth, went to the Royal Aircraft Establishment in December 1932, and was back at Gloster from August 1933 until it went again to the RAE for its last flight on 1 June 1934.

The striking Crusader seaplane designed by George Carter for the Schneider contest of 1927, on the Medway on 18 April, the day it was completed and launched at Shorts' Rochester factory. *(Bombardier Aerospace)*

Carter was also in charge of the third design, an extraordinary white elephant of an aeroplane, the lumbering three-engined DH72 Canberra biplane bomber. Work had begun at Stag Lane in mid-1927 to specification B22/27, before Carter joined the company, and the great aeroplane had languished in a hangar there through successive engine upgrades – it was powered by three Bristol Jupiters. Carter had the job of completing it and getting it into the air, which finally happened at Brockworth on 28 July 1931. The DH72's career was short-lived. It went to Farnborough in November and was abandoned the following August.

It seems that Carter's work at Gloster was confined to the de Havilland DH72 and DH77 projects. There is no evidence that he was involved in the design of the AS31, although he may have been engaged in facilitating the transfer from de Havilland. This was the period when Gloster's fortunes were at their lowest ebb – they built only a handful of aircraft between 1931 and 1933 and were saved from extinction by director Hugh Burroughes's proposal to the Air Ministry that the industry would be strengthened by merger. Hawker was riding high at the time, with massive orders for its Hart family of aircraft, and accordingly took over Gloster in February 1934. Carter became subordinate to his former deputy Sydney Camm, who was now in charge of all design work in the new group.

The following year Hawker's merger with Armstrong Siddeley formed the Hawker-Siddeley Aircraft Company Ltd and brought A.V. Roe of

Manchester into the group as well. Under the new management – with Burroughes now on the Hawker Siddeley board – Carter was sent north on secondment to work with Avro's chief designer, Roy Chadwick, at Woodford. He arrived in 1935 when design studies were beginning on the twin-engined Manchester bomber, forerunner of the famous Lancaster. This project was far more complex and demanding than anything Avro had tackled before. Their most recent military design was the Anson, one of the RAF's first monoplanes, which first flew in March 1935 and was itself a major technical advance over the little biplane trainers which were Avro's stock-in-trade.

Carter supervised the project design for the Manchester. His son, Peter, recalled in 2002: 'Chadwick got stuck – Father went to help him out a bit.' The first Manchester specification was issued the following year as P13/36. Carter returned to Gloster while the Manchester, designated Avro Type 679, did not fly until July 1939. It was not until January 1941 that its famous development, the Lancaster, first took to the air.

Carter took over as Gloster's chief designer at the beginning of 1937 when his outstanding predecessor Henry Folland resigned to set up his own company, as described in Chapter 1. Former Gloster designer Roff Jones recalled: 'I remember the stir that was caused in the [design] office when Folland left. Camm put a block on further development of Gloster aircraft.' According to Peter Carter, 'Camm wasn't very popular with my father.' Carter told Camm, his former subordinate at Hawker, that he too would resign unless he was made chief designer. Richard Walker, who joined Gloster from Hawker in January 1937 and became assistant chief designer to Carter, has left an intriguing note stating: 'W.G.C. kicked out by Camm and later found wandering round on a race meeting by H.K. Jones [a Hawker director] and offered a job at Gloster in place of Folland in 1936 or '37. F.S. Spriggs [Gloster's chairman] confirmed appointment of Carter and myself in London at the same time.'

George Carter in the early 1930s. (Peter Carter)

So Carter got the job and Gloster kept its own design department after all. He then got down to work and between 1937 and 1940 he embarked on a series of projects to various Air Ministry specifications.

The most promising of these was Carter's splendid Gloster G39, usually known from its specification number as the Gloster F9/37. Two of them were built, the very last piston-engined aircraft to bear the Gloster name (the E28 bore the company number G40). The design was a major revision by Carter of proposals which the company had already produced in response to specification F34/35 for a two-seater with remote-

The DH77 Interceptor in flight. *(A.J. Jackson Collection)*

George Carter photographed his wife Hilda beside Brockworth airfield, probably in 1931. Between hangars 1 and 2 are two Armstrong Whitworth Siskins, Carter's DH77, the Gloster Goring and Gorcock and what appears to be a Gloster Gamecock or Goldfinch. *(Peter Carter)*

Ahead of its time: Carter's de Havilland DH77 Interceptor J9771 in the New Types Park at the 1930 Hendon RAF Display, 'the only notable aerodynamic military advance of that year'. (A.J. Jackson Collection)

controlled gun turret, which in turn owed much to proposals for specification F5/33. The F9/37 is generally regarded as Carter's first design for the company. There is no evidence that he was responsible for any earlier designs in the period between the end of the DH72 saga and his transfer to Avro in 1935.

Like the E28 which was to follow it, the F9/37 was of all-metal stressed-skin construction but with fabric-covered control surfaces. Originally intended to carry a gunner operating a remote-controlled turret, it ended up as a single-seater with two 20mm cannon in the nose and a further four mounted dorsally behind the pilot, firing forward at an upward angle. Construction started in February 1938. The first to be completed, L7999, first flew at Brockworth on 3 April 1939, with Bristol Taurus engines and with Jerry Sayer at the controls. The following month it flew to Northolt for a high-speed demonstration at a top-secret air display specially staged for Members of Parliament, where it showed that it was capable of 366mph. It then went to the Aeroplane and Armament Experimental Establishment at Boscombe Down, where it received an excellent report but was damaged so badly after a few flights that it had to be returned to Gloster for repairs. This put back its development so severely that it did not complete its trials until July 1940, and although it was highly manoeuvrable and handled beautifully, neither it nor the second machine, fitted with Rolls-Royce Peregrine engines and serialled L8002, was chosen for production. Such was the secrecy of the project that no details were released until 1944.

Carter's F11/37 design was based on the F9/37, to be driven by more powerful Rolls-Royce Vulture, Armstrong Siddeley Deerhound or Bristol Hercules engines. The gunner was reinstated, with a turret which housed four 20mm Hispano cannon retracting flush with the fuselage in the down position, except for the gunner's head fairing. A bomber version of the design had a revised fuselage for carrying bombs or a torpedo. It was one of several contenders for a specification which ultimately resulted in the Bristol Beaufighter.

Carter was also working on another 1937 specification, F18/37, for which he prepared a novel twin-boom design with pusher propeller. This was the design, referred to at the end of Chapter 1, which particularly interested Frank Whittle when he was looking at the possibility of adapting an airframe already in development to flight-test his jet engine.

Other designs being developed at Gloster under Carter's leadership included a four-engined bomber to specification B1/39 as part of the Air Ministry's quest for the Ideal Bomber, a two-seater naval turret fighter

The lumbering de Havilland DH72 Canberra bomber, powered by three Bristol Jupiters, beside Gloster's Belfast hangars. George Carter transferred from de Havilland to Gloster with responsibility for completing and testing the DH72, a lengthy and unrewarding project.
(Roff T. Jones)

Forerunner of the famous Lancaster bomber of the Second World War: the Manchester bomber in early model and in prototype form. Seconded from Gloster, George Carter assisted Avro chief designer Roy Chadwick with the early stages of the project. *(Tony Buttler Collection)*

with some physical resemblance to Folland's earlier F5/34 single-seater, and a two-seat, twin-engined day and night fighter developed from Carter's F9/37 to specification F18/40. None of these was proceeded with.

At the beginning of February 1939 the drawing office held its second annual dinner. The menu showed a cartoon of the F9/37 gathering cobwebs; a dorsal bulge on the fuselage had a question mark over it – would it have a gun turret or not? Meanwhile, Gloster was building the Hawker Henley light bomber, but the production order was halved from 400 to 200, and it had been converted into a target tug. Hence the verses in the menu, which began:

> Pray silence Gentlemen awhile, there's something to relate,
> Of drawing office incidents of nineteen thirty eight,
> The F9/37 has been chopped and changed again,
> But luckily for all of us it's still an aeroplane.
> We hope that it will do its stuff, for we don't want to find
> It covered up with yellow paint and a drogue tacked on behind.

From this point Carter's work with Gloster is covered in the preceding chapters – Whittle's visit, the Air Ministry's invitation to design an airframe for Whittle's engine, the E28's first tentative flights at Brockworth and its subsequent career, and then the development of the F9/40 prototype and the Meteor – but this is a suitable place to complete the story. Assistant chief designer Richard Walker assumed full responsibility for the F9/40 programme in mid-July 1943. This left Carter free to work on new projects, including a jet fighter project for the Chinese Nationalist Government which involved a team of Chinese design engineers spending the best part of a year at Gloster between 1946 and 1947, before the project was abandoned for political reasons.

In 1947 George Carter was made a CBE for his work on jet aircraft and received the Royal Aeronautical Society's silver medal. The following year, when Richard Walker succeeded him as chief designer, he became Gloster's technical director – a sort of 'high priest', according to Hugh Burroughes, 'so that he could be thinking ahead and not be worried by day-to-day problems'. From 1954, in semi-retirement, he acted as technical consultant to the company, finally retiring in 1958. He lived up on Crickley Hill, overlooking the experimental department at Bentham and with the Brockworth airfield in the distance.

Gloster's last aircraft to enter production, the Javelin fighter, is usually described as Richard Walker's design, and he was indeed chief designer when it was built. But there is an intriguing reference in the unpublished memoirs of Gloster chief inspector Basil Fielding: his list of Gloster types ends with 'The Javelin two-seater delta wing all weather fighter designed by Mr R.W. Walker.' Alongside this there is a pencil note by Gloster's Javelin test pilot, Wg Cdr Dickie Martin: 'Basil – 3rd line from end – did RWW design the Javelin?' The words 'did' and 'design' are both underlined. This is followed by an ink amendment by Fielding: 'I think Mr Carter was the actual designer.'

George Carter photographed in his office by Russell Adams in the 1950s. Note the silver model of the E28/39 by his right elbow. *(Russell Adams Collection)*

Close-up of the silver model seen above. The base is inscribed: 'Presented to WG Carter CBE by the Hawker Siddeley Group to commemorate ten years of jet propelled flight 1941–1951.' *(Tim Kershaw)*

In May 1966, at the time of the twenty-fifth anniversary of the E28's first flight, a *Sunday Express* reporter tracked Carter down. He wrote:

The old man straightened up from the sweet peas in his Cotswolds garden and looked at the jet vapour trails in the sky above him. George Carter is 77 now and admits to being a 'pony and trap man'. Yet he is the pioneer who ushered in the jet age 25 years ago today. He designed the first jet – the Gloster-Whittle E28/39 – which made its test flight from Cranwell on the evening of May 15, 1941. Said Mr Carter: 'All sorts of rumours were current. Some thought it was a flying bomb and some people thought it would never get off the ground without a propeller.' The jet is now in the Science Museum. 'I haven't seen it for about 15 years,' said Mr Carter.

George Carter subsequently designed the Meteor and the Javelin to give Britain air supremacy in the first years after the war. But now he enjoys retirement on his 70 acres at Crickley Hill near Cheltenham –

In retirement George Carter was a familiar figure on horseback in the lanes below Crickley Hill, above Bentham. *(Peter Carter)*

and rides a grey mare called Linda. This year is his 50th wedding anniversary. His wife Hilda said: 'He sees few people from the old days. But I don't think they will ever forget what he has done.' Hawker Siddeley are to hold a dinner in London to celebrate the 25th anniversary of the first jet. George Carter will be guest of honour with Sir Frank Whittle, who built the engine.

Wilfred George Carter died on 27 February 1969 aged seventy-nine, survived by his wife, Hilda, and his son, Peter. Obituaries were published in *The Times* and the *Gloucestershire Echo*. Hawker Siddeley Aviation issued its own obituary of the jet pioneer. It concluded with a tribute from Hugh Burroughes, who had retired from the Hawker Siddeley Group board in 1966, fifty-seven years after entering the aircraft industry and fifty years after he had set up the Gloster company:

George Carter was a dedicated man in his career as an aircraft designer. Like many of his fellow designers he had to fight hard for success in a young but highly competitive industry. He was a reticent man, respected by his colleagues, but hardly recognised by the millions of jet travellers today as a major contributor to their freedom to move quickly and comfortably around the world. One of his most notable characteristics was the way he collaborated with Frank Whittle especially under the stress of war.

Eric Brown recalled that Carter and Whittle 'seemed to be very much at ease together'. He remembers Carter as a reserved and unassuming man, mild-mannered but with a quiet authority, who had a good relationship with his test pilots. Sid Dix recollects him as 'approachable'.

Carter's son and nieces remember a very kindly man with a great sense of humour and a twinkle in his eye – he was a great tease. He had a rather gruff voice and a short temper, though, and 'if he didn't like anything he'd up and go'. He was anything but a self-publicist – 'he never projected himself, ever'. They said that although he enjoyed spending time in the nearby Oddfellows public house with the Gloster test pilots, he was known for keeping his work and private life completely separate. He never liked flying himself and did not fly if he could help it.

George Carter expressed his views on the possible development of the jet in a chapter which he wrote for John Grierson's classic *Jet Flight*. Grierson gave Carter a copy of the book when it was published, inscribed:

> To George, who patiently suffered so much questioning and so much cajoling in the preparation of this book. I hope you will feel, as I do, that the effort of writing your chapter was well worth while, for it is one of the high-spots of the book. Although the role of a test-pilot may be to be taken on with high promises, to work hard for modest wages, and to be discarded without thanks, I shall always look back on my association with you and your colleagues at Bentham as one of the happy results of my profession. Wishing you even greater successes in the future in your struggle with the evil machinations of Herr Mach. Ever, John, 26.6.46.

Carter's chapter, entitled 'Trends of Development', was introduced by Grierson:

> The story, having started inevitably with Frank Whittle, the inventor and designer of the first jet engine, is rounded off by George Carter, the designer of the first turbo-jet aeroplane. Owing to George's natural modesty and retiring nature, it has been a struggle to induce him to raise his pen even in such a worthy cause, and I am indebted to Mrs Carter for her kindly persuasive influence. Unfortunately this important contribution is short, but it compactly summarises the future as seen by one of our leading aircraft designers. Readers will appreciate the obvious difficulty George has had to face in discussing likely developments without revealing secrets.

The text that followed is reproduced here in full:

> Jet propulsion has been accomplished by adapting the gas turbine to function as a propelling agent, a service for which it becomes increasingly suitable as the speed of flight is advanced. Another feature of the turbine is that it can be used just as well to drive a propeller, a device which will maintain high propulsive efficiency up to the speeds where the jet takes over. These two aspects have brought

the process of aeronautical development on to the threshold of an era with decisive possibilities.

Already the jet has made it possible to increase the flight speed more than could have been done with the conventional aero engine, and the time is not far off when speeds near to sonic velocity will be accomplished. The next step will be to pass through the sonic gateway and to emerge into a realm where flight exceeds the speed of sound. By that time the aeroplane as we know it today will have reached the final stage of evolution and development. But much remains to be done before that time arrives, and those who have predicted that supersonic flight speeds are in sight may have misapprehended some of the facts as these are understood at the present time. It may be accomplished before long with small types specially designed for research and experimental verification. But for those types to be planned for civil transportation it is a different story.

To give some idea of the price to be paid for speed, this small research aeroplane may be taken as an example. It would need to have very thin wings, a body just large enough to accommodate engine, fuel and pilot and nowhere to stow the undercarriage which presumably would be dropped after taking off. Assuming the drag of the aircraft to be 75lb at 100 miles per hour at sea level, its figure at the speed of sound at 30,000ft might be as much as 4,000lb, so that it would require about 7,250 horse power to fly at sonic velocity at that altitude. This seems to rule out supersonic speed except for military use where the price, whatever it may be, is never a matter of consequence.

Such considerations as the above suggest that a divergence will take place between those types suitable for very high speed in military service and those required for civil aviation. Certain classes of military aircraft, fighters for instance, which must achieve the highest possible emergency speed will have the jet engine installed in the fuselage. Perhaps the high speed unarmed bomber will make its appearance somewhat on the lines of a scaled-up version of the jet fighter. These military types, however, are in a specialised classification and their possible trend of development may not be freely debated at the present time.

Nevertheless this speed aspect is one which those concerned with the future development of aircraft suitable for civil aviation regard as specially interesting. Outstanding among civil aeroplanes, the long range express passenger-carrying type can best take advantage of the new means of applying the propulsive urge – the gas turbine with propellers. One day, transport machines also may be jet propelled, but this is hardly likely to be an immediate development. These heavy types have not yet been sufficiently improved and until a cruising speed of upwards of 400/450mph is in sight, they will not be ready for the jet engine. There is a long way to go before cruising speeds of this order can be accomplished commercially. About the best performance obtainable from civil transport at the present time is to cruise at 200/250mph, which is generally regarded as very much on the low side for a long journey. To advance progressively speed rather than size should be the order of the day and a future 30/40 tonner, cruising at an average of 400mph, makes an attractive target for early stages of development.

For the civil aeroplane the gas turbine driving propellers may be expected to make a significant contribution and there is little doubt that the day of the large petrol engine is now passing. There are good reasons why the turbine should supersede these large engines in certain future types for fast passenger-carrying aircraft, because the turbine is an incredibly simple device and can be developed to provide whatever shaft power may be required. As a power installation it has many virtues. It conforms to the elements of mechanical philosophy which requires that motion should be rotary rather than uni-directional. It makes use of low-grade fuel, eliminates vibration, requires no external cooling and for long and dependable operation should require little skilled attention. There is at present one notable drawback and that is the fuel consumption which compares unfavourably with the petrol engine. This aspect is most in evidence when the turbine is used for jet propulsion. But for the time being this question of fuel consumption is of little consequence when correlated with the advantage of exceptionally high speed.

Fortunately there is a marked improvement if the turbine is used to drive a propeller. Under these conditions, the thermal efficiency of the turbine is substantially enhanced, while the propulsive efficiency of the propeller is good so long as the speed of the aeroplane does not come within a specified margin of the speed of sound. Therefore, fuel consumption is unlikely to limit the effective use of the turbo-propeller or even of the jet installation so long as each functions within its own sphere.

As an alternative to the propeller, a ducted fan installation may be used in later stages of development, that is, when the speed has reached the high limit for reasonable propeller efficiency. These compounded installations are small diameter propellers working in an annular space surrounding the turbine. They are convenient for installation inside the fuselage, thus leaving the wings clear of bulging excrescences. It is too early to say how and to what extent ducted fans may influence the planning of designs. It all depends on the purpose behind the plan and until this has been clearly established, their possible association with a specific design assembly is not immediately to be foreseen. They may fulfil the requirements of an interim stage, turbo-cum-jet, having many commendable features when the speed of flight has not reached the condition suitable for the jet to do the job by itself.

Often questions are asked about the unorthodox types, such as those having the stabilising plane ahead instead of aft, those with tandem wing, and those usually referred to as all-wing or tailless arrangements. These different types have always attracted a good deal of attention and it is to be expected that interest will be revived even more actively now that the jet engine has arrived. The advantage of these unconventional aeroplanes is that they have no rear obstruction to get in the way of the jet. Other advantages are claimed and no doubt exist, otherwise their periodic renaissance would have been without meaning or purpose. The main point to establish is what quality may have been lost or compromised in diverting from the orthodox plan. This at the present time is almost exclusively represented by the conventional cantilever monoplane, a type in spite of its shortcomings generally regarded as the most satisfactory method of arranging the aerodynamic assembly. Behind it towers a vast background of knowledge and practical experience. This is always being expanded and while it is all to the good that progressive development should embrace any prospect of aerodynamic and structural improvement, it seems to be doubtful that these unorthodox types will immediately lead towards better aeroplanes than we have at the present time.

Summarising these brief impressions, it is greatly inspiring to look ahead and foresee the full implication of the new means of propulsion. That the gas turbine will enable us to travel by air a good deal faster than at one time was regarded as reasonably practicable is obvious. But for civil aviation, especially where passenger service is concerned, the outstanding need is to combine with speed the highest possible level of safety and reliability. Here again the vibrationless turbine marks a forward step. Now in the hands of the aircraft designer is a power unit which, with a propeller, will enable him to plan a safe reliable passenger vehicle, with noise and vibration almost entirely absent and a cruising speed double that of today's aeroplanes. At the same time in the military sphere, the jet opens up an entirely new vista of speed potential even beyond that of sound. Today we conclude the preliminary experiments. Tomorrow we look forward with well-founded confidence to the opening of a new era.

RICHARD WALKER

Dick Walker – Richard Walter Walker CEng FRAeS Hon MIED– was George Carter's number two, and played a leading part in the design of the E28. He was born on 27 December 1900 and from 1915, during the First World War, worked in the drawing office and works of the Universal Metallic Packing Company in Bradford. They specialised in general engineering, jigs, tools, machine tool design and steam engine accessories. He spent his last year there in charge of the design office, leaving in 1918 to join the newly formed Royal Air Force as an engine fitter. He left the service in 1920 to attend Bradford Technical College, where he obtained an Engineering Diploma research scholarship and became a part-time assistant lecturer in practical thermodynamics.

In 1924 Walker joined the Royal Aircraft Establishment at Farnborough as a draughtsman and detail stress calculator in the main design office. By 1925 he was in the design office of the Blackburn Aeroplane Company in Brough, but later that year headed south again when he was appointed chief technical assistant at Hawker Aircraft Ltd, Kingston upon Thames. He joined Hawker shortly before George Carter

Richard Walker at the age of seventeen, in mid-1918, the year he joined the Royal Air Force. *(A.K. Walker)*

left and Sydney Camm took over as chief designer. Camm's small technical staff consisted of E. Jones, Walker and Roy Chaplin, who were responsible for performance and strength calculations. By 1927 the Hart bomber was being built, Horsleys in squadron service were being modified, and design work on the new Hornet fighter – forerunner of the Fury – was under way.

Chaplin went on to become Camm's right-hand man, remaining so until he retired in 1962. Walker himself remained at Kingston until 1933, when he was transferred to Sweden for two years as personal assistant to the chief engineer and consultant to the Aircraft Department of AB Svenska Jarnvagonsverkestaderna, which later became SAAB. Here he was responsible for designing new aircraft types for the Swedish Government, introducing Hawker Harts and Ospreys into Swedish service and planning the building of Harts and Ospreys under licence. He was supervisor of the technical department in the design office. It was while he was in Sweden that he met his wife, Anna Kristina.

Walker was elected an Associate Fellow of the Royal Aeronautical Society in 1934 and he was back at Kingston in January 1935, appointed assistant designer at Hawker. On his return he told Camm, based on what he had seen in Sweden and Germany, that there was going to be a war, to which Camm replied, 'Don't be a bloody fool'. He was put in charge of early research on all-metal wings with stressed-skin covering which were destined for the new Hurricane monoplane fighter. He noted later: 'I was entirely responsible for the design [of the Hurricane's metal wing], directly to S. Camm at Hawkers, in 1935–36.'

By now Hawker had taken over the Gloster Aircraft Company, and when George Carter was appointed the new Gloster chief designer in 1937, Walker became his assistant chief designer and played a major part in the design of the E28. Before becoming involved with the E28, he was responsible for Hurricane production. He noted, 'I was used as a chaser for sub-contracts at various firms in the country,' and states that Gloster 'built ALL the metal wings for the Hurricane, peak rate sixty sets a week.'

Walker was heavily involved in the F9/40 project and was responsible for all Meteor development from July 1943, eventually succeeding Carter in 1948 and becoming Gloster's third and last chief designer, backed up by Reg Ward as his assistant. He became a Fellow of the Royal Aeronautical Society in 1949. He was responsible for the mighty Javelin delta-wing fighter which entered RAF service in 1954, and in the same year he was appointed technical director. He was also chairman of the Design-Production Committee controlling design for economy in production manufacture. In 1953 he was awarded honorary membership of the Institution of Engineering Draughtsmen and Designers. His F153D

thin-winged Javelin successor, four years in development, was scheduled to fly in July 1957 but was cancelled in 1956. Any hopes of further developments were dashed the following year, when the government announced that there would be no more manned fighters after the Lightning. After forty years, Gloster ceased to be one of the great designers and builders of RAF fighter aircraft.

Walter was appointed Technical Administrator of the parent company, Hawker Siddeley Aviation, in 1961 and when it closed Gloster in 1963, he transferred to Armstrong Whitworth in Coventry. When it in turn was closed in 1965 he headed north again, where he worked for Avro at Woodford until his retirement. He returned to his home in Cheltenham and died on 10 April 1982.

As chief designer for Gloster, Richard Walker poses beside a model of his Javelin jet fighter in 1952 or 1953. *(A.K. Walker)*

EIGHT

GLOSTER'S E28 PILOTS

Four Gloster test pilots flew the two E28s before testing was handed over to Farnborough: Jerry Sayer, Michael Daunt, John Grierson and John Crosby-Warren. Farnborough test pilot Eric Brown met Jerry Sayer 'only twice' but remembered him as 'very popular with other test pilots'. He described Daunt, Grierson and Crosby-Warren as 'great personalities' who worked well together. Test pilots then were essentially salesmen for their company's products, he said, which did not apply in the case of the E28. The Gloster pilots did not seem to be put out by the Royal Aircraft Establishment taking over their job and worked well with their counterparts at Farnborough.

JERRY SAYER

Britain's first jet pilot was Philip Edward Gerald Sayer, chief test pilot of the Gloster Aircraft Company. 'Jerry' or 'Gerry', as he was known, was a much loved figure who died in an aircraft accident – not in a jet – at the age of thirty-seven, some eighteen months after the E28 first flew.

Born in Colchester, Essex, on 5 February 1905, Sayer joined the Royal Air Force in 1924. As a young flying officer he served at Martlesham Heath, where all land-based aircraft were tested between the wars at the Aeroplane and Armament Experimental Establishment (AAEE). Aviation historian and former Westland test pilot Harald Penrose met him when he was attached to Westland for a short time, noting his good judgement and high skill as well as his 'vivid personality and infectious grin'.

Aircraft manufacturers at the time found it hard to train their own test pilots, so they were keen to employ RAF pilots who had served at Martlesham or the Royal Aircraft Establishment at Farnborough. The Air Ministry was willing to release test pilots who did not have permanent commissions, so when Hawker asked if Sayer could join them their request was granted. In 1930 he went onto the RAF reserve list and joined Hawker as number two to chief test pilot P.W.S. 'George' Bulman (not to be confused with Air Ministry official George Purvis Bulman). One of Sayer's fellow officers, Mutt Summers – brother of Gloster test pilot Maurice Summers – also left Martlesham at about this time, joining Vickers as their chief test pilot.

Hawker's trio of test pilots – Bulman, Sayer and Philip Lucas – became air-show favourites with the British public, displaying the Hart, the Fury and the Tomtit trainer with brilliant showmanship. Sayer's demonstrations of the Fury, particularly at the annual displays at Brooklands on Whit Mondays, were described as 'scintillating'. The three pilots also spent long periods abroad demonstrating the Hart bomber and Fury fighter to overseas customers. It was on his return from the Paris Aero Show in 1932 that Sayer had to be rescued from the Channel after the engine of Hart demonstrator G-ABTN failed.

Back at Brooklands, Sayer was pilot for a number of first flights. In 1931 he flew the first production Fury – the most elegant of all the RAF's biplane fighters – on 25 March; the Panther-engined version of the Hart on 21 May; the Hispano-engined version of the Yugoslav Fury on 27 August; and the first production Audax – the army cooperation version of the Hart – on 29 December. First flights in 1932 were those of the private venture Intermediate Fury on 13 April; the prototype Hart Trainer on 20 April; the second and third versions of the Wolseley-engined version of the Tomtit, on 11 August and 1 September; the Armstrong Siddeley Panther-powered version of the Norwegian Fury on 9 September; and the Dantorp version of George Carter's Horsley bomber on 19 September.

Sayer's last maiden flight for Hawker was that of the Hardy derivative of the Hart light bomber on 7 September 1934, the year that Hawker took over the Gloster Company. Sayer had been officially transferred the previous month, taking over from chief test pilot Howard Saint who had

The classic portrait: Jerry Sayer, Gloster's chief test pilot and Britain's first jet pilot. *(Flight)*

been with Gloster since 1927, back in the days of Folland's Grebe and Gamecock RAF fighters. (Saint retired from active flying in 1936 and was appointed manager of Doncaster airport. As a contracts officer in the space department at Farnborough, he finally retired at the age of seventy-two.) Sayer had already made several Gauntlet demonstration flights earlier in the year. Now, on 12 September, as Gloster's new chief test pilot, Sayer took the Gladiator fighter prototype, the SS37, into the air at Brockworth. Meanwhile, Gloster had received its first order from Hawker for the first production batch of twenty-one Hardys. Soon afterwards, on 17 December 1934, Sayer flew the first production Gauntlet.

Sayer went on to test Gauntlets and Gladiators, Gloster's last two biplane fighter designs. He flew the Gladiator prototype to Martlesham in early 1935 and the aircraft returned to Brockworth in mid-July for modification. He then undertook seven manufacturer's trials of the Gladiator in the next fifteen months, a total of 214 hours' flying. Roff T. Jones recalls: 'Often, during my apprenticeship years between 1937 and 1939, he would be airborne during our lunch breaks and would beat up Brockworth before landing for his own lunch at 1 p.m.' Sayer went on to take part in the development of the early Gloster monoplanes. The first of

these was Folland's F5/34, a much delayed and unsuccessful Spitfire and Hurricane rival, which Sayer first flew in December 1937.

By now Henry Folland had moved on to set up his own company, and George Carter had returned to Gloster from Avro, succeeding Folland as chief designer. Sayer was test pilot for the first Carter design built by Gloster, his F9/37 twin-engined fighter, making the first flight of the Taurus-powered F9/37 on 3 April 1939 and of the Peregrine-engined version on 22 February 1940. He was also heavily involved in testing the three Hawker monoplanes which were built by Gloster: the Hurricane, Henley and Typhoon. It was while testing an early Hurricane that he flew so low in fog that he scraped some trees and stripped fabric from the underside of the wings. He lived at Wistley Cottage, off the Cheltenham–Cirencester Road, up on the hill not far from the airfield.

As related in Chapter 2, Sayer was closely involved in the design of the E28 well before it flew, helping Carter plan the cockpit layout and visiting Power Jets at Lutterworth to take the controls of the W1 engine himself when it was running on the test bed. As an experienced test pilot he knew what he was doing in taking the E28 briefly into the air during its taxiing trials, even though the W1X engine was not passed for flight. The risk was small, as the aircraft only lifted into ground effect.

Sayer was a true pioneer of jet flight, piloting the E28 on all seventeen flights from Cranwell, between 15 and 28 May 1941, and on its next ten flights, all from Edge Hill. In the long intervals between E28 test flights – the E28 was grounded between the end of May 1941 and mid-February

1942 – he was busy testing production Typhoons rolling off the assembly line at Brockworth. Gloster had already built 500 of them and was now into its third production batch of 700, building two dozen aircraft a week. Sayer was also closely involved in the development of the Gloster F9/40 – the forerunner of the Meteor fighter – and from 10 July 1942 carried out taxiing trials in a prototype with de-rated W2B engines. He advised: 'The engines must not leave the ground', adding that it was 'recommended that engines of more thrust should be made available for the first flight of this aeroplane'. Although he had been briefly airborne on 10 July, the project was put on hold until more powerful engines became available and the first flight proper of a Meteor did not take place until 5 March 1943, after Sayer's death.

Sayer with production test pilot Maurice Summers beside a Gloster-built Hawker Henley. *(Jet Age Museum Collection)*

John Grierson wrote: 'He spent a great deal of his time at the design office in conference with Carter, Yardley, Walker, James and Lobley concerning lessons learnt on the E28 and problems to be tackled in the next project.' He added that after Sayer was appointed OBE in the 1942 New Year's honours list, it seemed 'incongruous . . . that the management did not see fit to make him a director. . . . He did so much administrative work in the running of the firm, that many people thought he actually was a director, but when asked about this he always smiled and said, "I suppose it would cost them an extra £100 a year for director's fees."' The award citation recognised his work as a test pilot but made no mention of jet flight – the very existence of the E28 would not be announced until two years later, on 7 January 1944.

Sayer's last flight in the E28 was on 27 September 1942 (p. 49). His death, on 21 October, while testing a Typhoon, was a great shock to his colleagues. *Flight* photographer John Yoxall wrote within days: 'As a test pilot he was outstanding, and it is regretted that security reasons preclude us from giving details of what he has been doing since the outbreak of hostilities.' He continued:

Anyone who knew 'Gerry' Sayer loved him. It was impossible to do otherwise. His infectious smile and gentle humour were always present. I never knew him to be worried or 'under the weather' however difficult or dangerous a task on which he might be employed.

While at Brooklands he frequently flew me in the old Hawker Hart G-EBMR, when I was photographing Hawkers' latest products in the hands of Flt Lt Bulman. They formed the perfect team, each trusting the other completely, and it was a revelation and joy to fly with such pilots.

Joseph Whiteley of Gloucester was quick to pen a dire tribute in verse, dated 24 October, which began 'We knew him not, and yet, we knew him well, / We denizens of Gloucester . . .'

A memorial service was held in Gloucester Cathedral on the last day of the month. The announcement read: 'No Flowers. Contributions will be accepted for the endowment of a bed in the Cheltenham General Hospital, and should be sent to the Secretary of the Gloster Aircraft Company. Any Surplus will be sent to the Royal Air Force Benevolent Fund.' Writing to the local paper years later, F.J. Revell, a retired chief inspector of aircraft, recalled 'He was a wonderful pilot, honest and a real gentleman, and it was an honour to have known him.'

Maybe the most heartfelt tribute of all came from John Grierson in *Jet Flight*. 'There never has been and probably never will be a finer type of chief test pilot than Jerry, who combined such a high degree of personal charm and leadership with an unequalled skill in the handling of an aeroplane.' He recalled the memorial service, when Gloucester Cathedral:

> was filled by hundreds of work-people from the Gloster factory, by RAF officers and by representatives of the aircraft industry from all parts of England. The Bishop of Tewkesbury read the funeral service for one who lay buried in the depths of the sea, to be followed by the last act of devotion by the men of Glosters, an act which was in its effect terrific, because it was so sincere and so unexpected. Quite unheralded, the works' male choir filed out in front of the assembly and in conjunction with a soloist in the gallery sang 'The Holy City'. This was the great and final tribute. . . . In the esteem of all the test pilots in this country, Jerry held a unique position.

Grierson dedicated his classic work to Sayer's memory, quoting a young poet, D.R. Geraint Jones, who at the age of twenty-two in June 1944 was fatally wounded in Normandy: '. . . Your monument / Abides, wrought not in stone or clay / But in the lives of those whose gain / Was knowing you. For with you went / A joy too deep for words to say / That left a wound too deep for pain.'

MICHAEL DAUNT

Neil Michael Daunt, known to all as Michael, was born in Hastings on 23 October 1909. His first flight – in 1919, at the age of nine – was a five shilling joyride over his home town, flying with his mother in Navarro's war-surplus Avro 504K.

After learning to fly in the Cambridge University Air Squadron, Daunt joined the RAF in 1930 and served in 25 Squadron as a member of its renowned aerobatic team, flying Fury biplane fighters tied together in formation and getting to know the Hawker trio of Bulman, Sayer and Lucas at Hendon air displays. Completing his short service commission, he became an instructor at the de Havilland Flying School at Hatfield in 1935. Bulman invited him to join Hawker the following year, to his great

delight; he was transferred to Gloster in 1937 as a production test pilot under Jerry Sayer and as a colleague of Maurice Summers.

Most of Daunt's early work involved flying Gladiators, which were being ordered in quantity for the RAF and winning valuable overseas orders for Gloster as well. By November 1937 a total of twenty-six Gladiator Mark Is had been shipped to Latvia and a further fourteen to Lithuania. Daunt went out soon afterwards with a works team to instruct the two air forces. He took over as a production test pilot on Henleys and Hurricanes in 1939, and in early 1940 was in Portugal testing Gladiators for the Portugese Air Force. He was also briefly employed testing Albemarle bombers which were coming off the assembly line of A.W. Hawkesley in No. 2 Factory on the other side of Brockworth airfield.

As senior assistant test pilot, Daunt was present at the E28's taxiing trials in April 1941 and at the first Cranwell flight on 15 May. There is no official photograph of this momentous event, and it was Daunt with his camera who provided the only visual record of the occasion – he said later: 'If I had a pound for every time those pictures have appeared in newspapers, magazines and books since then I would be a very rich man.'

Although E28 flight testing at Cranwell continued until 28 May, Daunt returned to Brockworth early in order to make the first flight of the first Gloster-built Hawker Typhoon, R7576, on 27 May. He continued to be closely involved with the Typhoon programme.

Later, testing production Typhoons, his oil tank emptied itself at 25,000 feet. He made a forced landing in a field in ground mist, severing both wings between two trees. Describing the Typhoon as 'one of the most bloody ever', he said that 'the things that went wrong with it before it went to the RAF were appalling'. After trying for some time to get some trees at the end of the runway felled in case of engine failure on take-off, he wrote to Gloster works manager Frank McKenna:

First flight of a jet pioneer: Michael Daunt, aged nine, and his mother before taking off on a five shilling joyride over Hastings and St Leonards in 1919. The war-surplus Avro 504 still carries its service serial D9304. *(Michael S. Daunt)*

Michael Daunt visited Latvia in 1937 to supervise the handover of twenty-six Gladiators to the Latvian Air Force. *(Michael S. Daunt)*

Production of the Typhoon began in 1941. The first Gloster-built Typhoon was flown by Michael Daunt on 27 May, the same day that Jerry Sayer was piloting the E28 on its fourteenth and fifteenth flights at Cranwell. EK288, shown here, was a 'car door' type Typhoon 1B of Gloster's third production batch of 700 aircraft.
(Jet Age Museum Collection)

I wish to God that I could see
A gap where now doth stand a tree,
A tree that now is bearing nuts
May, one day, bear some pilot's guts.
Please, Mac, don't wait for MAP,
Just give us space and not a tree!

The Folland 'Frightful' almost
cost Michael Daunt his life
when it broke up in mid-air on
19 May 1942. *(Tim Kershaw
Collection)*

Although Henry Folland had left Gloster in 1937, in 1942 he almost
became Daunt's nemesis. The Folland Aircraft Company had produced a
flying engine test bed in 1940, the Folland 43/37. The first two were
assembled at Eastleigh, the remaining ten at Staverton (now
Gloucestershire Airport), very close to Brockworth. Folland had asked
Gloster if they could provide a test pilot. Sayer and Daunt both disliked
the lumbering, fixed-undercarriage monoplane and Daunt quickly named
it the 'Folland Frightful'. He drew the short straw, and on 19 May 1942,
when he was flying from Staverton to conduct diving trials, P1777 broke
up and scattered itself along 2 miles of fields near Tewkesbury. Daunt's
harness gave way, and he was thrown through the cabin roof and landed
– still holding his parachute ripcord – with broken wrist and collarbone,
and partly strangled. First on the scene was the local vicar. Daunt
recalled: 'The doctors told me that if you are slightly strangled, you tend,
when you come to, to be violent and . . . I clocked this poor little man
who had been doing his good Samaritan act.' Daunt kept the ripcord as a
souvenir, using it as the lavatory chain pull at home.

John Grierson wrote that when he, Sayer and McKenna visited Daunt, 'still delirious, in Tewkesbury Hospital, we thought he would never be able to fly again'. He was off flying for five months, at a crucial time in Gloster's own activities, and the company withdrew its pilots from testing the 43/37. In October 1942 Daunt regained his flying licence and, after Sayer's untimely death, he now became chief test pilot himself. As Britain's second jet pilot, he flew the E28 for the first time from Edge Hill on 6 November 1942, a week after the memorial service for his colleague. After three more flights at Edge Hill he accompanied the E28 to Farnborough, where RAE test pilot H.J. Wilson – later to set a world speed record in a Meteor IV – took over to continue tests with the W1A/3 engine.

It was on 27 January 1943 that Daunt almost lost his life again. He was standing in front of the port engine nacelle of F9/40 DG206 during ground running of the engines at Bentham. Whittle's account says that, bending forward to check for fuel leaks, Daunt was sucked head first into the intake. Four ground crew were unable to free him until the engine was stopped. Badly bruised and shaken, but not otherwise injured, he was off work for two days and it affected him for a long time afterwards. It was after this that 1 in square steel-mesh grilles were fitted in jet engine intakes, known to the Gloster ground staff as Anti-Daunts and at Power Jets as Daunt Stoppers. Whittle wrote: 'I hope Michael Daunt will forgive me if I mention that he was no feather-weight, and the fact that he could be whipped off his feet into the intake was an indication of the very powerful "vacuum cleaner" effect if one got too close.' Richard Walker commented: 'Exaggeration. I was standing a few feet away and waved down the engineer in the cockpit to shut down the engine immediately. Michael had the presence of mind to bend his arm so [he] went in elbow-first and was saved by his grip on the intake entry rims, i.e. only one arm and a part of a shoulder were sucked in.'

Daunt flew E28 W4041 fourteen times in all, from Edge Hill, Farnborough, Brockworth and Barford. He also flew the second E28, W4046, four times between 16 and 20 April 1943. On 19 April he was at the controls of W4046 for a short demonstration flight in front of Prime Minister Winston Churchill at Hatfield. John Grierson wrote that Daunt 'stole the show', flying past at 400mph, some 50mph faster than the Spitfires and Mosquitoes there. 'The story went around that the Prime Minister, in swinging round in order to follow the course of the Pioneer, had to move so quickly that he very nearly spilt his whisky and soda.' Air Ministry director of engine development George Bulman presented Daunt to Churchill after 'a superb display' lasting 11 minutes. He recorded that the Prime Minister asked Daunt many questions, thanked him for his magnificent display and gave him a large cigar. Daunt flew the aeroplane back to Edge Hill the following day; the flight took just 24 minutes.

His last E28 flight, on 14 June 1943, was in W4041. He had already taken over F9/40 taxiing trials from Sayer and made the first flight, in the H1-powered fifth prototype, at Newmarket on 5 March 1943. He also piloted five of the other seven F9/40 prototypes on their first flights. It was on one F9/40 test flight that an impeller disintegrated and Daunt

Michael Daunt in retirement visited the firm of Henry Wiggins which developed the high-temperature alloys used in Whittle's jet engines. He is holding two turbine blades and a photograph of the first E28 signed by several of the people who worked on it. *(Michael S. Daunt)*

managed to crash-land successfully in a potato field. The aircraft was promptly nicknamed the 'Whittle-Daunt Potato Lifter' and Daunt remarked that the potatoes 'were chipped and cooked as well as delivered'. On another occasion, Sid Dix remembered, Daunt put a Meteor down on the sands at Westbury-on-Severn.

Meteor testing and development was a long, slow process with many discouraging results. It was after suffering aileron flutter and high-frequency vibration of the control column during a dive from 20,000 feet that Daunt wrote a short verse for George Carter:

> Sing a song of shock-stall, words by Ernest Mach
> Four and twenty slide-rules, shuffling in the dark
> Begone, O doubting fancies, our George will fill the bill
> But George! Please make the Meteor a wee bit meatier still.

Daunt was appointed OBE for his work in 1944, resigning from Gloster later in the year with a reputation for thoroughness and accuracy. He took up farming in Oxfordshire and reported that his colleagues remarked, 'Oh yes, Mike – he's now spreading it as well as talking it.' Eric Greenwood took his place as Gloster's new chief test pilot.

An unidentified press cutting from 1966 begins:

A nationwide search has tracked down a man who helped make aviation history – then disappeared. After countless false leads Michael Daunt – second man to fly Britain's first jet plane – was found in the quiet Devon town of Bideford. The SOS had been sent out by executives of the Hawker Siddeley combine who next week will celebrate the 25th anniversary of the aircraft.

Referring to the circumstances of his succeeding Sayer, he was quoted as saying 'Jerry Sayer was a very good friend of mine', adding, 'Believe me this wasn't a case of who is the next brave man – everyone was dying to get their mitts on that aircraft.'

Between 1969 and 1976, in his sixties, Daunt worked as chief technician of the Wordsley Hospital kidney unit in Stourbridge. He died in July 1991 at the age of eighty-one.

JOHN GRIERSON

Gloster test pilot John Grierson, the first man to fly the second E28, was born in 1909. In 1928, at the age of nineteen and with practical jet flight well in the future, he met Frank Whittle when his first term at RAF Cranwell coincided with Whittle's last. One day – it was 31 May – Whittle asked Grierson to run him to Newark railway station in the sidecar of his motorcycle, a powerful Brough Superior, which Grierson did at maximum speed to get there in time. On arrival, a shaken Whittle told him: 'Tomorrow will be my twenty-first birthday. I was told by a fortune-teller that I should not live to be twenty-one; I thought this was it.'

On leaving Cranwell, Grierson joined the elite 12 (Bomber) Squadron at Andover, whose 175mph Fairey Fox day bombers were the fastest aircraft in the RAF. It was then that he first met Jerry Sayer, who had just joined Hawker and who gave Grierson a ride in Hawker's new, even faster Hart. Grierson's pre-war career was altogether more spectacular than Sayer's or Daunt's. In the autumn of 1930, posted to 11 (Bomber) Squadron at Risalpur in India, he flew out in a third-hand de Havilland Moth, G-AAJP.

A young John Grierson poses beside his de Havilland Gipsy Moth *Rouge et Noir* during his flight to Samarkand in 1932.

Rouge et Noir, now on floats for Grierson's Arctic air route attempt of 1933, seen on the Blackburn slipway at Brough on 27 July. *(A.J. Jackson Collection)*

Grierson's de Havilland Fox Moth G–ACRK, *Robert Bruce*, seen on the Medway at Rochester before his epic flight to Ottawa and New York in 1934. *(A.J. Jackson Collection)*

It was painted red on one side and black on the other and christened *Rouge et Noir*. The following May, wanting to make the most of his annual leave, he flew the Moth back to England in a record-breaking 4 days, 10 hours and 30 minutes, landing at Lympne on 28 May and making the headlines in the national press. He was twenty-two.

In August 1931 Grierson flew an RAF padré to Baghdad and back, landing twice in the desert to ask the way. Then, in 1932, after a brief flight to Finland, he made a 9,000-mile flight to Astrakhan and Samarkand, describing his experiences in *Through Russia by Air* (1933). The following year saw his first attempt, with *Rouge et Noir* now on floats, to explore the Arctic air route to North America. 'People said that I was mad . . . they thought my crash and lucky escape in Iceland would teach me a lesson, and it did, but not the one they thought. With a bigger and better aeroplane, the *Robert Bruce*, I set off over London in 1934.' He became the first man to fly from England to Canada.

The *Robert Bruce* was a de Havilland Fox Moth equipped with floats and registered G-ACRK. It took off from the Medway at Rochester on 20 July. The longest leg, from Londonderry to Iceland, took ten hours. 'After another crash in Iceland and a night out in Greenland, [I] reached my twin objectives – Ottawa and then New York.' He had taken 61 hours' flying time to reach Ottawa, arriving on 30 August. No one in New York knew he was coming and the airport mechanics refused to believe he had crossed the ocean. The flight inspired his second book, *High Failure* (1936). He concluded that the Arctic route was too difficult to open up, but a few years later, in the Second World War, American Lend-Lease equipment was flown to Britain via airfields in Greenland and Iceland. 1936 was also the year that he married Frances Hellyer, who accompanied him on some of his flights.

Grierson's first job as a test pilot appears to have been with Armstrong Whitworth, for whom he was involved in testing the lumbering Whitley bomber. He had a hair-raising experience when stalling a Whitley at high altitude, managing to land safely but with one engine broken up, the nose hatch blown in and fabric torn from the starboard wing. He became a Hawker pilot in 1940, testing repaired Hurricanes at Cowley, Oxford. Colleague Alex Henshaw, who later became chief test pilot at the Castle Bromwich Spitfire factory, described him as 'a quiet, serious, modest Scot'. Not only had he painted his famous aircraft red and black – all black seen from the port side, all red from starboard – but he had painted his car in the same way. Henshaw wrote: 'This flamboyancy was I felt quite out of keeping with John's normal quiet character.'

In 1941 Grierson joined Gloster, working as a production test pilot on Hurricanes and Typhoons until he became Daunt's number two on the E28 team in 1943. As the third member of the Gloster jet test pilot team, he became the first man to fly W4046 when it made its 11-minute maiden flight from Edge Hill on 1 March 1943. He was to fly it thirteen more times in March and April, before it went to Farnborough at the beginning of May and remained there until Davie's crash in July. He made the first cross-country E28 flight on 17 April 1943, flying the E28 from Edge Hill to Hatfield, for Michael Daunt's demonstration to Winston

John Grierson in the cockpit of the first prototype Meteor F Mk I, EE210/G, at Muroc Lake in the United States in 1944. A Bell P–59 Airacomet – the first US jet aircraft – came to Britain in exchange and was based at Moreton Valence.

Churchill two days later. The following month saw him take up W4041 for the first time, from Brockworth on 27 May, after it had returned from Farnborough and been fitted with the newer W2/500/3 engine. By the time he made his last flight, from Barford on 25 June, he had flown W4041 fifteen times. With a total of twenty-nine E28 flights in his logbook, he had overtaken Sayer's twenty-seven flights and Daunt's eighteen.

Grierson went on to play a significant part in the development of the F9/40 and Meteor, including a lengthy visit to the United States. He piloted DG208, powered by Rolls-Royce W2B/23 Welland engines, on its first flight on 20 January 1944 from Moreton Valence, and DG207, powered by Halford H1b (Goblin) engines – the prototype Meteor F2 – on its first flight on 24 July 1945, also from Moreton Valence. This was his last flight for Gloster. He left soon afterwards, delivering DG207 to de Havilland at Hatfield in September for engine tests. After serving in the British Zone of Germany as deputy director of civil aviation, he worked for de Havilland from 1950 to 1962.

Grierson now began work on another major contribution to the history of Britain's first jet: his wonderful book *Jet Flight*, published in 1946. It is so well informed and so readable that it seems extraordinary that it has never been reprinted. In the introduction Grierson relates the story of carrying Frank Whittle in his sidecar and observes: 'My claim to authorship is therefore unique. Unlike the many "fathers of jet propulsion" who advance arguments good or bad to prove that without their ingenuity jet propulsion could never have been developed, I alone can claim to have been within a measurable distance of having stopped the whole process before it had ever started.' He went on to write several more books on aviation and Polar exploration: *Air Whaler* (1949), *Sir Hubert Wilkins: Enigma of Exploration* (1960), *Challenge to the Poles: Highlights of Arctic and Antarctic Aviation*, with a foreword by Charles A. Lindbergh (1964) and *Heroes of the Polar Skies* (1967).

Grierson lived in the Channel Isles in retirement. He died in May 1977 at the age of sixty-eight, after suffering a heart attack while delivering a talk at the National Air and Space Museum in Washington DC as the main speaker in a symposium on the fiftieth anniversary of Charles Lindbergh's flight from New York to Paris. His last book, *I Remember Lindbergh*, with an introduction by Anne Morrow Lindbergh, was published later that year.

JOHN CROSBY-WARREN

Standing in front of F9/40 DG205/G are (left to right) John Crosby-Warren, Michael Daunt, Gloster general manager Frank McKenna, Frank Whittle and George Carter. This was the aircraft in which Crosby-Warren was to lose his life on 27 April 1944. *(Russell Adams Collection)*

Youngest and least well known of Gloster's four E28 pilots, John Crosby-Warren was instantly recognisable because of his great height. He flew both E28s a total of five times in all, and was killed in a prototype Meteor accident in 1944.

Crosby-Warren was born in Bristol in 1911. He joined Gloster in 1940 and was a production test pilot on the Henleys, Hurricanes, Typhoons and Albemarles built by the company. Aviation historian Henry Matthews

describes him as gregarious and 'a very fine professional pilot' with 'many years experience on all types of aircraft', and says that because of his height he had to do without a cushion under his parachute in order to fit into a Typhoon. He became an experimental test pilot on the E28/39, F9/40 and Meteor. His first E28 flight was in the second aeroplane, W4046, on 13 March 1943 from Edge Hill. John Grierson wrote that 'he miraculously packed his six feet eight and a half inches into the rather limited accommodation of the E28 cockpit'. He flew it again the following day and on 3 May took it on its third cross-country flight, from Edge Hill to Farnborough, where it remained for the rest of its career. Squadron Leader Douglas Davie, who did most of the flying on W4046 at Farnborough, accompanied Crosby-Warren in a Spitfire. Crosby-Warren wrote: 'In order to keep behind and in formation with the Spitfire, I had to fly with such a small throttle opening that the undercarriage horn was on most of the time and the rpm were only 13,000 or just over.'

Gloster test pilot John Crosby-Warren photographed by his colleague Michael Daunt.

A few weeks later Crosby-Warren made two flights in the first E28, W4041. Both were on 26 June 1943 from Barford and were the aeroplane's sixty-ninth and seventieth flights. W4041 did not fly again until 9 March 1944, by which time it too was based at Farnborough, where it remained until it was retired in February 1945. With both E28s gone, Crosby-Warren became fully employed on testing the F9/40 and Meteor.

John Grierson relates that 'a successful, but somewhat dogmatic, designer of fighters with "up-and-down" engines was against the development of the jet, as being too far off in its eventual application to be of any real use in this war'. The designer asked Crosby-Warren, 'What is the use of embarking upon a high level fighter like the F9/40 when the whole trend of war is to fight lower and lower?' Crosby-Warren replied: 'As a matter of fact, owing to the absence of airscrews, we find that it is possible to fly a jet machine lower without touching the ground than a propeller-driven one.' It seems highly probable that the designer was the famous Sydney Camm, chief designer of Gloster's parent company, Hawker, and creator of the Hurricane and Typhoon. As the Gloster test pilots knew only too well, the Typhoon had been a failure as an interceptor but had come into its own as a ground-attack fighter.

Crosby-Warren took over the Meteor prototype DG206 for development flying and also spent many hours flying DG205. It was in this aeroplane that he was the first pilot to suffer an engine failure in flight, at the beginning of July 1943. On 27 April 1944, again in DG205, an external mass balance came off when he was diving over Minchinhampton, not far from Moreton Valence. He was killed when the aircraft hit the ground upside down and disintegrated. It was shortly after his thirty-third birthday.

NINE

COMMEMORATING THE PIONEERS

The achievement of designing, building and flying Britain's first jet has been commemorated in a great variety of ways. Whittle received a knighthood and Carter was appointed CBE. Experimental department manager Jack Johnstone was made an MBE. H.W.V. Steventon's daughter Janet recalled in 2003 that the members of the Gloster drawing office involved with the E28 were awarded a single MBE citation between them. They drew lots and it was won by Reg Ward.

After its last flight on 20 February 1945, W4041 went to Bentham in March to be refurbished and repainted by Gloster (albeit in a colour scheme which is not authentic) so that it could go on public display in London between 21 June and 16 September, as part of the Ministry of Aircraft Production's Britain's Aircraft Exhibition on the site of the bombed-out John Lewis department store in Oxford Street. It then went back to Gloster and was displayed in King's Square in Gloucester and in the Promenade in Cheltenham, before being presented on 27 April 1946 to the Science Museum in London, where it was put on permanent display. It now hangs in a place of honour and is one of the most significant aircraft in the museum's collection. Whittle's W1 engine is on show separately nearby. The museum also shows on continuous loop a film about the early development of jet engines and aircraft, in which the E28 features prominently.

The E28 did, however, leave the Science Museum briefly in 1951, when it was the centrepiece at a commemorative dinner on 31 May at the Dorchester Hotel in London, organised by Hawker Siddeley 'honouring the first ten years of jet powered flight in the free world'. Guests at the top table were Thomas Sopwith, Frank Whittle (by now Air Commodore Sir Frank Whittle KBE CB MA DSc FRS HonMIMechE FRAeS), George Carter, marshals of the Royal Air Force Sir John Slessor and Viscount Trenchard, and Maj Gen Leon W. Johnson of the United States Air Force. Several of the pioneers whose names have featured in this book were there: Hugh Burroughes, Sydney Camm, John Cuss, Michael Daunt, George Dowty, Robert Feilden, Ivor James, W.E.P. Johnson, Jack Johnstone, Jack Lobley, Frank

Three rare photographs of W4041 in The Promenade, Cheltenham, probably in April 1946, an event which seems to have been ignored by the local newspaper at the time. *(Russell Adams Collection)*

W4041 newly refurbished by Gloster before going on public display. *(Russell Adams Collection)*

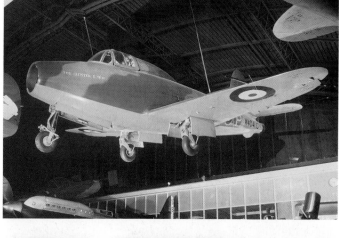

W4041 as first displayed in the Science Museum, South Kensington, with undercarriage lowered. *(Russell Adams Collection)*

Whittle's original W1 jet engine in the Science Museum in 2002. *(Tim Kershaw)*

George Carter speaking at the Hawker Siddeley dinner held in May 1951 to commemorate 'the first ten years of jet powered flight in the free world'. Frank Whittle is seated on the right. *(Russell Adams Collection)*

On a less formal note, three unidentified men pose on the E28 at the Hawker Siddeley dinner. *(Russell Adams Collection)*

McKenna, H.W.V. Steventon, Richard Walker and Gp Capt H.J. Wilson. Sid Dix recalled, though, that 'Bill Baldwin and the rest of us were not told anything about it, which annoyed us.'

It was on this anniversary that Carter was presented with a gold cigarette case inscribed 'To Mr W.G. Carter, commemorating the 10th Anniversary of The First Flight of the Gloster Whittle E28/39 on 15.4.41. May 1951. T.O.M. Sopwith. Frank S. Spriggs.' He was also presented with a silver desktop model of the E28 by the Hawker Siddeley Group.

Frank Whittle has been the subject of countless books, articles and programmes, and the first flight of the E28 – the first flight at Cranwell, that is – appears in the record books and has been featured on postage stamps and first-day covers. Carter's significance has been overshadowed by Whittle's undoubtedly greater achievement, but as well as his 1947 CBE, he was honoured fifty years later, in June 1997, when he was featured on a 43p stamp issued by the Royal Mail in its Architects of the Air series, designed by Turner Duckworth of Chiswick. Inappropriately, the stamp showed a Meteor T7 trainer – Carter's classic jet indeed, but in a version that had been developed by Richard Walker from Carter's original design.

In the Gloucester and Cheltenham area today a brass model of the E28 is displayed in Cheltenham's Regent Arcade, commemorating its completion in the Regent Motors Garage which was demolished to make way for the shopping centre. The model was made and presented by apprentices of the Dowty Group, which made the E28's landing gear. Regent Motors in fact stood a little further down Regent Street, past the Everyman Theatre, on the site where BhS stands today. For many years a commemorative plaque was displayed in the Regent Motors showroom. It was unveiled in the presence of former Gloster experimental manager

Right and above opposite: First-day covers marking the thirtieth anniversary of the rarely commemorated first Brockworth flight and the fortieth anniversary of the first Cranwell flight. *(Jet Age Museum Collection)*

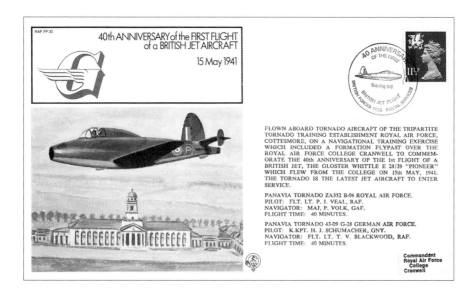

RAF FF30
40th ANNIVERSARY of the FIRST FLIGHT
of a BRITISH JET AIRCRAFT
15 May 1941

FLOWN ABOARD TORNADO AIRCRAFT OF THE TRIPARTITE TORNADO TRAINING ESTABLISHMENT ROYAL AIR FORCE, COTTESMORE, ON A NAVIGATIONAL TRAINING EXERCISE WHICH INCLUDED A FORMATION FLYPAST OVER THE ROYAL AIR FORCE COLLEGE CRANWELL TO COMMEMORATE THE 40th ANNIVERSARY OF THE 1st FLIGHT OF A BRITISH JET, THE GLOSTER WHITTLE E 28/39 "PIONEER" WHICH FLEW FROM THE COLLEGE ON 15th MAY, 1941. THE TORNADO IS THE LATEST JET AIRCRAFT TO ENTER SERVICE.

PANAVIA TORNADO ZA352 B-04 ROYAL AIR FORCE.
PILOT: FLT. LT. P. J. VEAL, RAF.
NAVIGATOR: MAJ. P. VOLK, GAF.
FLIGHT TIME: 40 MINUTES.

PANAVIA TORNADO 43-09 G-28 GERMAN AIR FORCE.
PILOT: K.KPT. H. J. SCHUMACHER, GNY.
NAVIGATOR: FLT. LT. T. V. BLACKWOOD, RAF.
FLIGHT TIME: 40 MINUTES.

Commandant
Royal Air Force
College
Cranwell

Jack Johnstone MBE, who was in charge of the teams at both Regent Motors and Crabtree's Garage. Johnstone's daughter was also there. She had worked in the office at Crabtree's and often made tea for Whittle when he made his many visits to the screened area where his W2B engine awaited installation in W4046.

A similar plaque once hung in reception at Simon Gloster Saro, the last incarnation of the Gloster name, on Gloucester Trading Estate. It is now part of Jet Age Museum's collection.

Elsewhere in Cheltenham, in Carlton Street, there is a plaque on the wall of the former Crabtree's Garage. It reads: 'Cheltenham Civic Society. The second prototype British jet aeroplane the Gloster/Whittle E28/39 was assembled in this building 1942–43. British Aerospace.' Credit for the erection of the plaque goes particularly to James A. Benn MRAeS. It was unveiled on 25 March 1995 by Tony Casson of British Aerospace. Those present included Lord Kings Norton, Dr Geoffrey Bone and Dr Robert Feilden. Lord Kings Norton reminded those present of the very important role played by George Carter.

In Gloucester the E28 is one of eight Gloster-built aircraft featured in the neglected 'aviation garden' in Constitution Walk behind the Museum and Art Gallery. There is also a statue in Northgate Street, 'Spirit of Aviation' by Simon Stringer, which commemorates the achievements of the Gloster Aircraft Company, including the E28. Some way south of the city centre, in Shakespeare Avenue in Podsmead, Lower Tuffley, there is the splendidly named Jet and Whittle public house. Successive owners renamed it the Red Rooster and the Double Gloucester, but in 2001 the Jet and Whittle name was reinstated.

At Brockworth itself all that survives is the former No. 2 Factory to the east of Golf Club Lane, behind the more recent façade of Dupont UK Ltd. The main Gloster site is still being developed as Gloucester Business Park, but until the turn of the twenty-first century much of the factory survived as Gloucester Trading Estate. No. 3 Hangar, which housed the experimental shop, was demolished in the early 1990s. The final Belfast

Dowty apprentices' brass model of the E28 in Cheltenham's Regent Arcade. The BhS store now stands on the Regent Motors' site. (*Tim Kershaw*)

hangar, No. 1, nearest the road, was the last of the Gloster buildings to survive on the main site, finally being demolished in 2002.

A feature of the trading estate was a plaque sculpted by Anita Lafford on a plinth by the main gate. It bore a low-relief image of the E28 in flight, and read:

> The Gloster E28/39. First British jet aircraft. Designed and constructed by Gloster Aircraft Company Ltd, a member of the Hawker Siddeley Group, on this site in 1940–41 and powered by the first jet engine invented by Sir Frank Whittle. This plaque is also a tribute to all GAC personnel who contributed so much to the 1939–45 war effort. Commemorative plaque designed by Gloster Design Services (c & b) Ltd.

Beneath the plaque, on the stone plinth made by John Hopkins, was inscribed 'Presented by Hugh Burroughes Esq CEng FRAeS, Director of the Gloster Aircraft Company 1917–1966'. The full significance of the plaque's unveiling in 1979 was noted under the headline 'First jet honoured at last' in the *Daily Telegraph*. The paper's air correspondent, Air Cdre E.M. Donaldson, wrote on 24 May: 'After an unexplained lapse of 38 years, one of the most important top secret technical battles of the Second World War – the fight to get the world's first jet-engined aircraft into the air – was commemorated yesterday . . .'

This commemorative plaque hung in Simon Gloster Saro's premises on the Gloucester Trading Estate and is now part of Jet Age Museum's collection. A similar plaque, with the additional words 'in these premises' was formerly displayed in the showroom of Regent Motors in Cheltenham. (*Tim Kershaw*)

The former Crabtree's Garage in Carlton Street, Cheltenham, in 2003, together with the local Civic Society's commemorative plaque, which can be seen on the front wall. *(Tim Kershaw)*

The original Jet and Whittle pub sign in Lower Tuffley, Gloucester. *(Russell Adams Collection)*

THE GLOSTER E28/39

FIRST BRITISH
JET AIRCRAFT

DESIGNED AND CONSTRUCTED BY
GLOSTER AIRCRAFT COMPANY LTD.
A MEMBER OF THE HAWKER SIDDELEY GROUP
ON THIS SITE DURING 1940-41 AND POWERED BY THE FIRST
JET ENGINE INVENTED BY SIR FRANK WHITTLE

THIS PLAQUE IS ALSO A TRIBUTE TO ALL G.A.C. PERSONNEL WHO
CONTRIBUTED SO MUCH TO THE 1939-45 WAR EFFORT

Commemorative Plaque Designed by Gloster Design Services (c&o) Ltd.

This plaque, which once stood at the entrance to the Gloucester Trading Estate, has been re-erected by Arlington at the heart of their Gloucester Business Park. Both the Gloucester Trading Estate and the Gloucester Business Park were built on the site of the Gloster factory airfield. *(Tim Kershaw)*

All that survives of the Gloster factory airfield at Hucclecote and Brockworth: buildings of the A.W. Hawkesley factory, on the former No. 2 Site, are now part of Dupont nylon spinners. *(Tim Kershaw)*

Leylandii have replaced the original elm trees which once disguised the water tower of the former Gloster experimental department at Bentham. *(Tim Kershaw)*

Camouflage paint can still be seen on the main shed at Bentham, shown earlier in the background of the photograph of F9/40 DG204/G (page 59). *(Tim Kershaw)*

This E28 replica, built by the Sir Frank Whittle Commemorative Group, stands on a traffic island in Lutterworth, Leicestershire, near the original Power Jets works. It was unveiled by Ian Whittle, Sir Frank's son, in May 2003. *(The Sir Frank Whittle Commemorative Group)*

DG202/G, the first F9/40 prototype, on display at the Aerospace Museum at Cosford. *(Roger Wallsgrove)*

The plaque was removed by business park developers Arlington when the site was cleared. It has now been re-erected beside the business park's central water feature, but there is no longer any reference to Hugh Burroughes's generosity.

The old Gloster experimental department at Bentham remains largely intact and is the most complete survival of the area's deep involvement with the development of jet flight. Most of the sheds at Moreton Valence survive, too, but the former airfield is bisected by the M5 motorway, which follows the line of the old runway.

The Midland Air Museum in Coventry has a display devoted to Frank Whittle, who was born in the city on 1 June 1907.

Two fibreglass replicas of the E28 have been moulded for the Sir Frank Whittle Commemorative Group, which assembled and finished them at the Rolls-Royce factory at Ansty, just outside Coventry. One is on public display on a traffic island at Lutterworth, home of Whittle's Power Jets works, where it was unveiled by Frank Whittle's son Ian in May 2003 (ironically, it is Carter's airframe which commemorates Whittle's engine). The other was built to go on show at Farnborough, where the two E28s did so much of their test flying at the Royal Aircraft Establishment. It was unveiled by former Rolls-Royce chairman Sir Ralph Robbins in September 2003. Jet Age Museum plans a third replica, as described below.

Archive material relating to Whittle and the E28 is held in the National Archives, formerly the Public Record Office, at Kew, under AIR62 (the Whittle papers) and by the Science Museum. Whittle's own papers are deposited with Churchill College, Cambridge. Grainy black and white film footage of the taxiing trials at Brockworth, believed to have been taken by Michael Daunt, is in the Huntley Film Archives in London. M.L. Nathan's colour footage of the E28 at Farnborough, apart from featuring in the Science Museum display, can be seen on the video *Meteor, The Ultimate Profile*, a Leading Edge production for DD Video in 2000.

Meteor prototype DG202/G, after many years in the open air quietly deteriorating as 'just another Meteor', was finally given due recognition. It was restored and is now on display in the Cosford Aerospace Museum in Shropshire.

JET AGE MUSEUM

There is one other major source of information and archive material, Jet Age Museum, without which this book would not have been possible. Jet Age is devoted to saving and commemorating Gloucestershire's aviation heritage and is currently seeking support from the Heritage Lottery Fund to build a permanent home. It is run by Gloucestershire Aviation Collection, a registered charity, which was set up by a group of volunteers mostly from the Cheltenham and Gloucester area after a public meeting held in Cheltenham in 1986.

The museum will soon start work on a full-scale model of the E28 as the focal point in its proposed new building. The original in the Science Museum hangs out of reach with its wheels up and its cockpit canopy closed.

The only known relic of the E28 outside the Science Museum is this nose wheel, donated to Jet Age Museum by Bill Baldwin's son John in 1998. *(Tim Kershaw)*

Jet Age's replica will stand on its undercarriage with the cockpit fitted out and open for inspection by museum visitors. It will based on a third set of glass fibre mouldings from masters created by the Sir Frank Whittle Commemorative Group. The project has been made possible by generous donations from the Reactionaries, a group of more than fifty men and women who worked on the early development of the jet engine, and a grant from Tewkesbury Borough Council.

Jet Age is the museum of the Gloster Aircraft Company and of Gloucestershire's aviation heritage. Its core collection consists of aircraft and artefacts, documents and photographs relating to Gloster, Dowty and Smiths. All three main versions of the Gloster Meteor are represented. As well as the cockpit of an early Meteor F3 fighter (the fourth oldest British jet to survive after the E28, the F9/40 prototype and another F3 cockpit section) there are four complete Meteors: an F8 fighter, two T7 trainers and an NF14 night fighter. The collection also includes a Gloster Javelin FAW9 currently on display inside the main entrance to Gloucestershire Airport at Staverton. A fully-detailed reproduction of the Gloster Gamecock biplane fighter of 1925 has been constructed by the museum's own volunteers from construction drawings recreated by another team of members. A Gloster Gladiator II fighter shot down in Norway in 1940 is being rebuilt by museum members from wreckage generously donated by the Norwegian government. The museum also has a small collection of other classic jets.

Jet Age Museum first opened to the public in Unit 2B on the Gloucester Trading Estate, the former Gloster factory site, in 1994. Its distinguished patrons include such jet pioneers as Dr Robert Feilden, Captain Eric 'Winkle' Brown RN and Lady Kings Norton, whose late husband was head of the National Gas Turbine Establishment which the British government set up to coordinate jet engine development. It relocated to Hangar 7 at Gloucestershire Airport in 1996, still hoping to return to Brockworth, and it was then that Sir Frank Whittle himself wrote:

I have heard of the work of the Gloucestershire Aviation Collection, of which two of my war-time colleagues in the development of the jet engine are now Patrons. The progress which has already been made in building up wide-ranging collection of both airframes and engines is most encouraging, and I am impressed by the fact that, subject to adequate funding being available, a permanent home can be found for the Collection at the site where the first British jet aircraft did its taxiing trials, during which it made some short flights. I should like to commend the Gloucestershire Aviation Collection's application for funds from the Heritage Lottery Fund, as the proposed Museum will provide a permanent reminder of a most important stage in the development of jet aircraft in the United Kingdom.

The collection had to go into storage at the end of 2000 so that the airport site could be redeveloped, and not long afterwards plans for the Brockworth site had to be changed, but the museum's tenacious volunteer membership has kept the project alive. Most of the building blocks for achieving a permanent home for the collection are now in place. Tewkesbury Borough has pledged £250,000, Gloucester City and Cheltenham Borough have promised a one-hectare site at the airport and outline planning permission has been granted. At the end of November 2003 the Heritage Lottery Fund agreed to give Jet Age up to £15,700 as 90 per cent of the cost of developing the design of the new building and producing an access and audience development plan. This will be used to prepare the museum's main funding application for building a permanent home at the airport.

Jet Age archives house the remarkable collection donated by Bill Baldwin's son John in 1998, which includes the original spare nosewheel and tyre from the E28 as well as priceless documents and photographs. The museum is also responsible for the management of the unique Russell Adams Collection which has been used extensively for this book. Adams was the Gloster Company photographer and the pioneer of jet air-to-air photography.

Museum members are far from idle, even though the collection currently remains in storage. The main bid for Heritage Lottery Fund support will soon be submitted. Meanwhile, volunteers are conserving and developing the Russell Adams Collection, rebuilding the Gladiator and fundraising; work will soon start on the E28 replica.

Jet Age Museum deserves to succeed. By achieving a permanent home for the collection it will make a major contribution to commemorating Britain's first jet propelled aircraft and the men and women who designed, built and flew it.

TEN

AFTERWORD

The development of military jet aircraft has been astonishing, but the real difference to our everyday lives has been made by long-distance air travel. The jet age proper could be said to have begun not in April or May 1941, but on 2 May 1952, when a British Overseas Airways Corporation de Havilland Comet jet airliner first flew with fare-paying passengers. Two years later the Comets were grounded by a series of fatal accidents, but they had clearly shown that jet flight was the way ahead: fast, comfortable, quiet, vibration-free, efficient and increasingly affordable. International air travel on the scale we know today would have been impossible with the propeller-driven airliners of earlier years.

In more than fifty years of jet travel, attitudes and values have changed too. The technical advances represented by the Comet and the later supersonic Concorde were hailed by press and public with the sort of jingoistic overkill that now seems appropriate only to jubilees and World Cup victories. Jet aircraft contribute to global warming as their aerial blowtorches heat up the world's atmosphere, and airports cover thousands of green acres with runways, while mass travel brings vast car parks, bank holiday hell, environmental overload of once-unspoilt destinations and the rapid global spread of disease.

Jet flight is a mixed blessing, but on balance it has given us more than it has taken away. And it all stems from those early years in Gloucester and Cheltenham – and in Germany. This is where the history becomes somewhat tangled. Frank Whittle is acknowledged as the inventor of the world's first practical gas turbine for aircraft propulsion – the jet engine – and it was indeed Britain which gave the new technology to both the United States and the Soviet Union. But others had been working on jet flight, too. Whittle's patent had been published in a German magazine, and the world's first jet aeroplane first flew in Germany in 1939. This was the Heinkel He 178, powered by a gas turbine invented by German engineer Pabst von Ohain.

Both Britain and Germany developed jet aircraft in great secrecy as the contribution which jet propulsion could make to the war effort was eventually recognised. It is highly unlikely that either side knew what the other was doing until the first jets entered the war: Germany's Messerschmitt Me 262 and Britain's – George Carter's – Gloster Meteor. The two types never met each other in combat, although the Me 262 was used to attack Allied bombers and the Meteor proved effective against

German V1 flying bombs in the later stages of the war. The technology was so secret that both sides had to confine jet operations to their own airspace to prevent their aircraft falling into enemy hands.

The secret of jet flight was made public in a joint RAF and US Army Air Force announcement on 7 January 1944, stating that a British jet-propelled aircraft had successfully passed experimental tests and that both Britain and America had production of such aircraft in hand. The British authorities were keen to portray it as a British invention brought about by British genius. This was true enough, although it ignored the way the Government had treated Whittle and it downplayed German developments, suggesting that they were a dead end which came to an abrupt halt when Germany was defeated.

In truth, German research and development was far advanced. It was thoroughly evaluated by the Allies and made a major contribution to Allied development of the jet, to an extent which is hard to assess. Many German scientists and technicians, too, continued their work after the war's end, notably in the United States and the Soviet Union, but in other countries too.

It is still reasonable to state that the jet engine was Whittle's invention and that the engine he developed was the forerunner of every jet flying today. This was the engine which first left the ground near Gloucester in April 1941. That it was able to do so was made possible by the major contributions of George Carter, Jerry Sayer and the men and women of the Gloster Aircraft Company, Gloucestershire's jet pioneers.

APPENDICES

THE E28 IN DETAIL

A THE E28'S VITAL STATISTICS

Span 29ft. Length 25ft 3in. Height over cabin 7ft 2in and over rudder 9ft 3in. Track 7ft 10in. All-up weight 2,886lb empty; 3,691 or 3,748lb loaded according to source.

Main planes: Aerofoil GW2 special high-speed Piercy section, 12 per cent thick at root tapering to 9 per cent thick at tip. N-type (high lift) wings: NACA 23012 at root tapering to 23009 at tip. Dihedral on chord line 4 degrees 12 minutes. Chord root 7ft, wing tip (projected) 2ft 7in. Incidence 1 degree. Dihedral on chord line 4 degrees. Aileron span 5ft 10.6in. Aileron chord (max) 15.2in.

Tail unit: tailplane including elevators, span 12ft. Chord (max) 3ft 4in. Incidence 1¾ degrees. Elevators: span 12ft, chord (max) 15.52in.

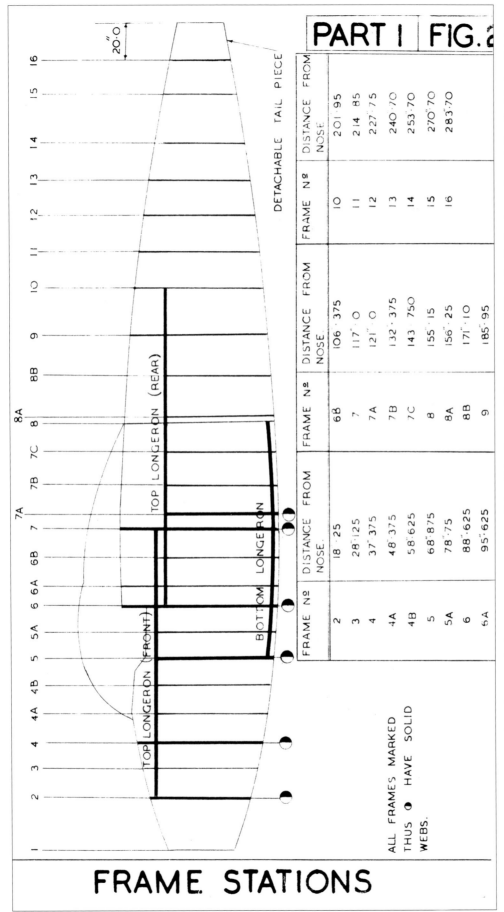

PART 1 | FIG. 2

FRAME STATIONS

DETACHABLE TAIL PIECE

20.0"

TOP LONGERON (FRONT)

TOP LONGERON (REAR)

BOTTOM LONGERON

ALL FRAMES MARKED
THUS ● HAVE SOLID
WEBS.

FRAME Nº	DISTANCE FROM NOSE.	FRAME Nº	DISTANCE FROM NOSE.	FRAME Nº	DISTANCE FROM NOSE.
2	18·25	6B	106·375	10	201·95
3	28·125	7	117·0	11	214·85
4	37·375	7A	121·0	12	227·75
4A	48·375	7B	132·375	13	240·70
4B	58·625	7C	143·750	14	253·70
5	68·875	8	155·15	15	270·70
5A	78·75	8A	156·25	16	283·70
6	88·625	8B	171·10		
6A	95·625	9	185·95		

Key to the E28's fuselage frames, from the original Gloster Company Prototype Notes. Note: the overall dimension of 303.70m is for the fuselage only, excluding the jet pipe. (Jet Age Museum Collection)

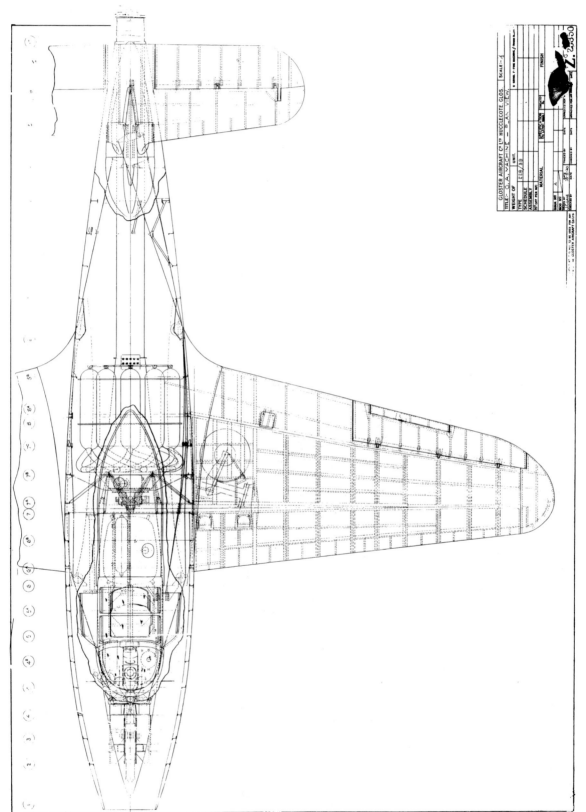

Above and opposite: Detailed elevation and plan views of the E28/39 dating from August 1940, from original Gloster glass plate negatives. *(Jet Age Museum Collection)*

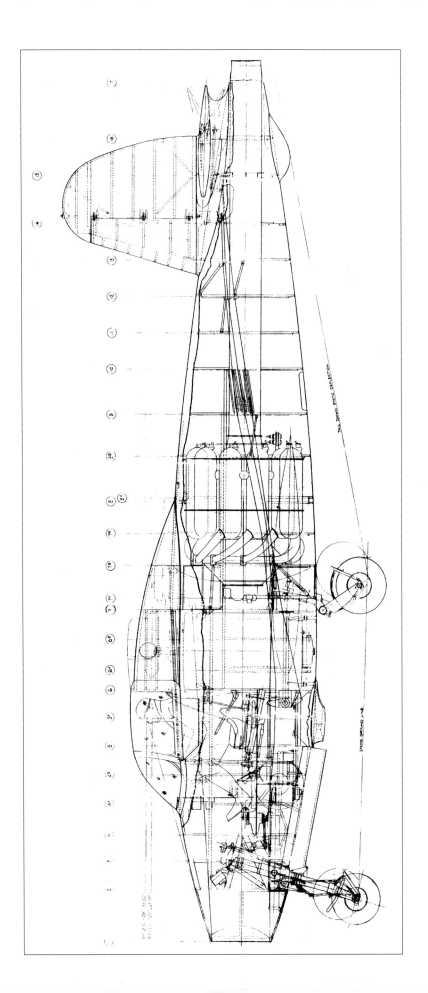

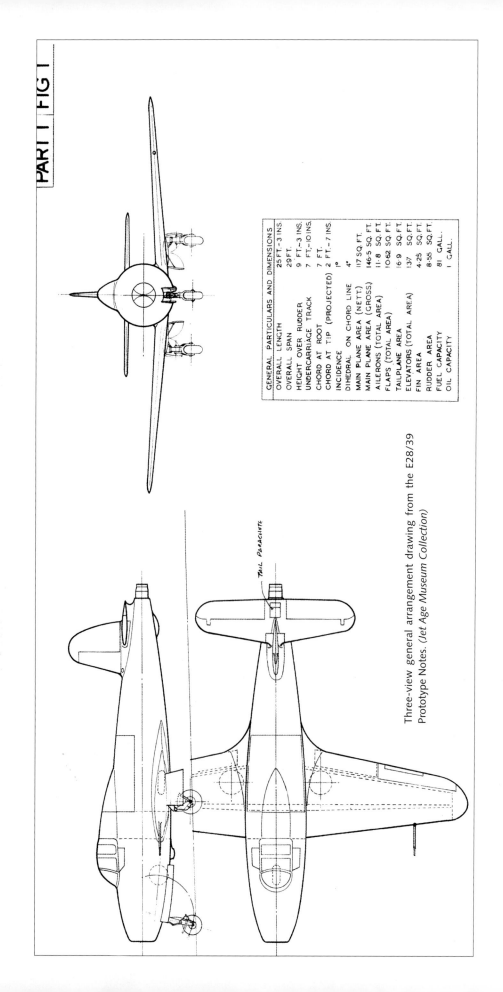

GENERAL PARTICULARS AND DIMENSIONS	
OVERALL LENGTH	25 FT.–3 INS.
OVERALL SPAN	29 FT.
HEIGHT OVER RUDDER	9 FT.–3 INS.
UNDERCARRIAGE TRACK	7 FT.–10 INS.
CHORD AT ROOT	7 FT.
CHORD AT TIP (PROJECTED)	2 FT.–7 INS.
INCIDENCE	1°
DIHEDRAL ON CHORD LINE	4°
MAIN PLANE AREA (NETT)	117 SQ. FT.
MAIN PLANE AREA (GROSS)	146·5 SQ. FT.
AILERONS (TOTAL AREA)	11·8 SQ. FT.
FLAPS (TOTAL AREA)	10·62 SQ. FT.
TAILPLANE AREA	16·9 SQ. FT.
ELEVATORS (TOTAL AREA)	13·7 SQ. FT.
FIN AREA	4·25 SQ. FT.
RUDDER AREA	8·55 SQ. FT.
FUEL CAPACITY	81 GALL.
OIL CAPACITY	1 GALL.

TAIL PARACHUTE

Three-view general arrangement drawing from the E28/39
Prototype Notes. *(Jet Age Museum Collection)*

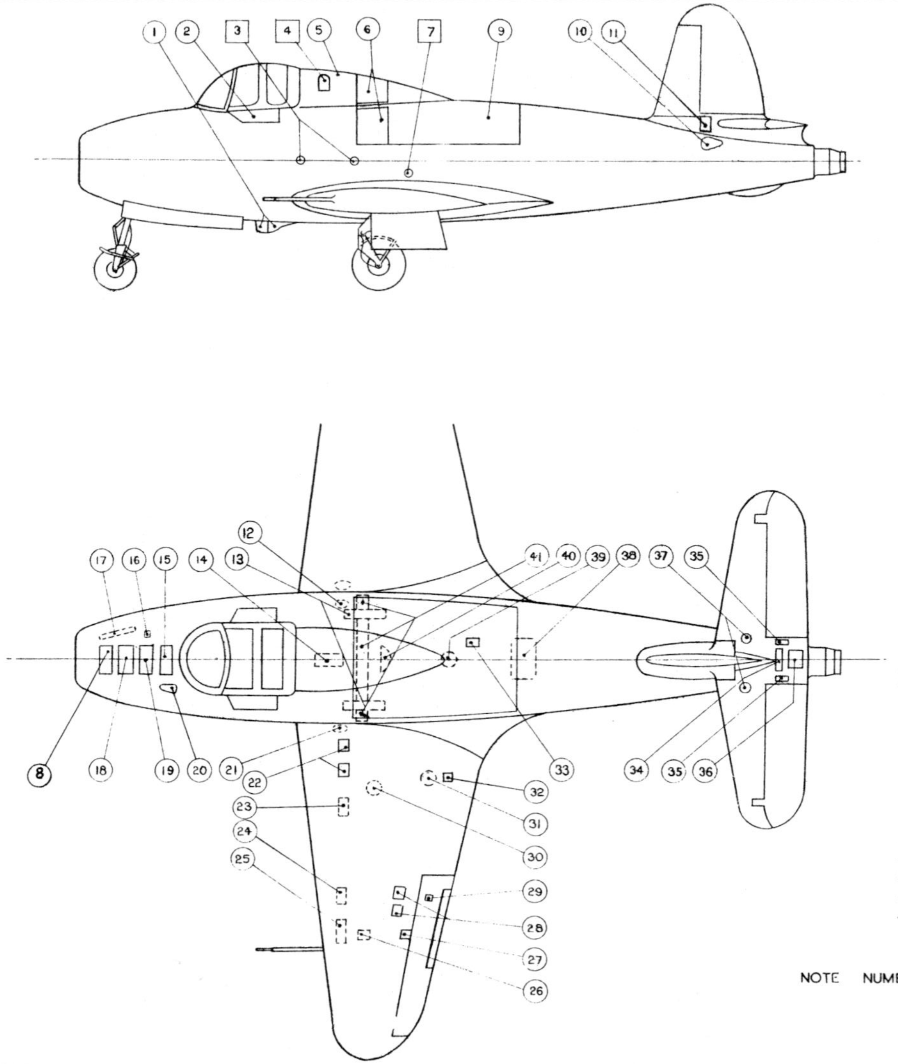

1 ACCESS TO VENTURI TUBE
2 DOOR FLAP
3 DATUM POINTS
4 ACCESS TO FUEL TANK FILLER CAP
5 TANK DOOR
6 ACCESS TO FRONT OF POWER UNIT
7 SOCKET FOR STARTER LEADS
8 ACCESS TO BALLAST WEIGHTS
9 ENGINE DOOR
10 RUDDER & ELEVATOR LAY SHAFTS & JET PIPE SUSPENSION LINK
11 RUDDER SHAFT
12 AILERON TORQUE TUBE SPROCKET
13 BOTTOM LONGERON JOINT PLATE
14 ACCESS UNDER TANK
15 ACCESS TO BACK OF INSTRUMENT PANEL
16 ACCESS TO HYDRAULIC RESERVOIR FILLER CAP
17 AIR THERMOMETER
18 BALLAST WEIGHTS & NOSEWHEEL MECHANISM
19 NOSEWHEEL MECHANISM & HYDRAULIC COMPONENTS
20 ACCESS TO BACK OF INSTRUMENT PANEL
21 AILERON CONTROLS
22 AILERON CONTROLS & ADJUSTERS
23 AILERON CONTROL FAIRLEADS
24 AILERON CONTROL SPROCKET & ADJUSTERS
25 AILERON CONTROL TORQUE TUBE & PITOT HEAD
26 TORQUE TUBE JOINT
27 AILERON TOGGLE ARM
28 ACCESS TO AILERON MASS BALANCE
29 BALANCE TAB OPERATING GEAR
30 ACCESS BETWEEN SPARS
31 FLAP JACK PIPES
32 FLAP JACK
33 ACCESS TO OIL TANK FILLER CAP
34 ACCESS TO TAIL PARACHUTE CONTROL BOX
35 PARACHUTE DOOR JETTISON PINS
36 PARACHUTE DOOR
37 ACCESS TO PARACHUTE MECHANISM
38 MANHOLE DOOR
39 ACCESS UNDER ENGINE
40 ACCESS TO BOTTOM FRONT OF ENGINE
41 ACCESS TO MAIN PLANE TO FUSELAGE JOINT

NOTE NUMBERS SHOWN IN SQUARES □ ARE PORT ONLY

REMOVABLE DOORS AND PANELS

Key to removable doors and panels from the Prototype Notes. (Jet Age Museum Collection)

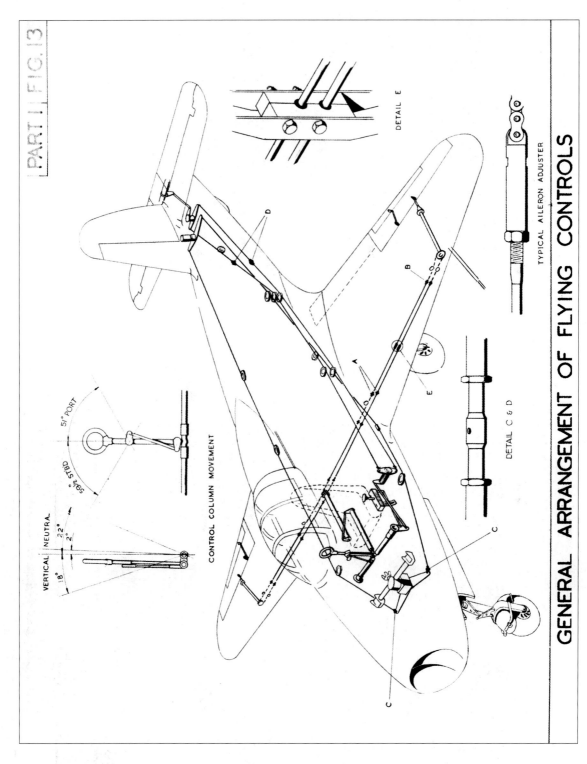

DETAIL E

TYPICAL AILERON ADJUSTER

DETAIL C & D

5I° PORT

56½° STBD

VERTICAL NEUTRAL.

22°

18°

2°

CONTROL COLUMN MOVEMENT

A

B

C

C

D

D

E

GENERAL ARRANGEMENT OF FLYING CONTROLS

General arrangement of flying controls from the Prototype Notes. *(Jet Age Museum Collection)*

B THE COCKPIT

A general view of the E28's cockpit, March 1941. The air intake ducts have not yet been fitted. (© Crown Copyright/MOD)

The starboard (left) and port sides of the cockpit before the ducts were fitted, March 1941. (© Crown Copyright/MOD)

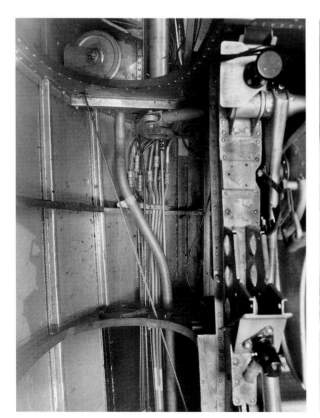

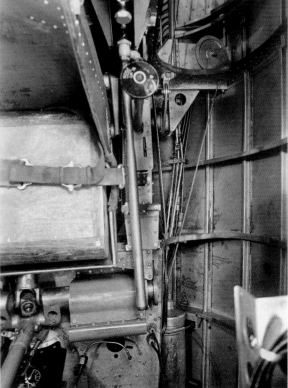

Two views of the cockpit in
November 1940 before
installing the seat and the
instrument panel. *(© Crown
Copyright/MOD)*

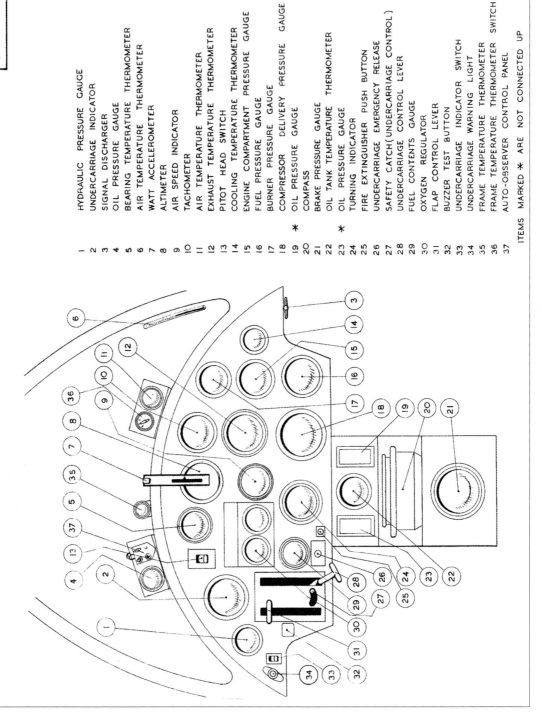

PART. I. | FIG. 3.

1	HYDRAULIC PRESSURE GAUGE
2	UNDERCARRIAGE INDICATOR
3	SIGNAL DISCHARGER
4	OIL PRESSURE GAUGE
5	BEARING TEMPERATURE THERMOMETER
6	AIR TEMPERATURE THERMOMETER
7	WATT ACCELEROMETER
8	ALTIMETER
9	AIR SPEED INDICATOR
10	TACHOMETER
11	AIR TEMPERATURE THERMOMETER
12	EXHAUST TEMPERATURE THERMOMETER
13	PITOT HEAD SWITCH
14	COOLING TEMPERATURE THERMOMETER
15	ENGINE COMPARTMENT PRESSURE GAUGE
16	FUEL PRESSURE GAUGE
17	BURNER PRESSURE GAUGE
18	COMPRESSOR DELIVERY PRESSURE GAUGE
19	OIL PRESSURE GAUGE *
20	COMPASS
21	BRAKE PRESSURE GAUGE
22	OIL TANK TEMPERATURE THERMOMETER
23	OIL PRESSURE GAUGE *
24	TURNING INDICATOR
25	FIRE EXTINGUISHER PUSH BUTTON
26	UNDERCARRIAGE EMERGENCY RELEASE
27	SAFETY CATCH (UNDERCARRIAGE CONTROL)
28	UNDERCARRIAGE CONTROL LEVER
29	FUEL CONTENTS GAUGE
30	OXYGEN REGULATOR
31	FLAP CONTROL LEVER
32	BUZZER TEST BUTTON
33	UNDERCARRIAGE INDICATOR SWITCH
34	UNDERCARRIAGE WARNING LIGHT
35	FRAME TEMPERATURE THERMOMETER
36	FRAME TEMPERATURE THERMOMETER SWITCH
37	AUTO-OBSERVER CONTROL PANEL

ITEMS MARKED * ARE NOT CONNECTED UP

General Layout of Instruments from the E28/39 Prototype Notes. *(Jet Age Museum Collection)*

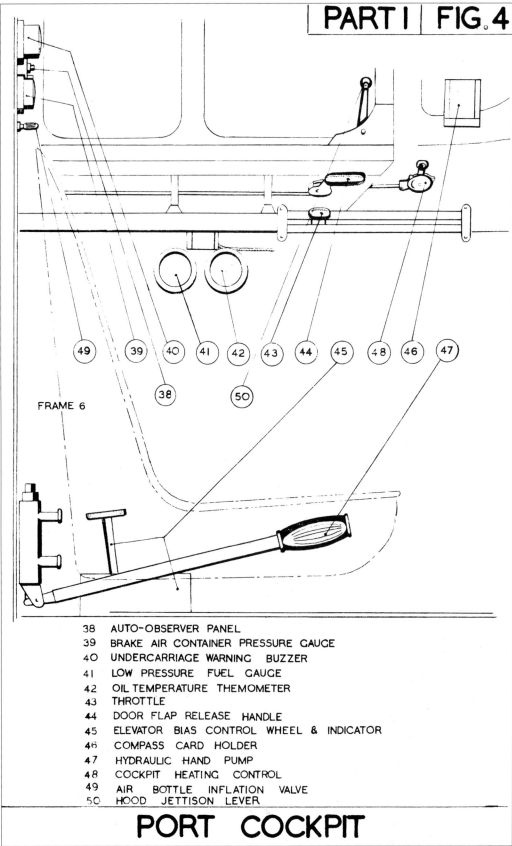

PART I | FIG. 4

FRAME 6

38	AUTO-OBSERVER PANEL
39	BRAKE AIR CONTAINER PRESSURE GAUGE
40	UNDERCARRIAGE WARNING BUZZER
41	LOW PRESSURE FUEL GAUGE
42	OIL TEMPERATURE THEMOMETER
43	THROTTLE
44	DOOR FLAP RELEASE HANDLE
45	ELEVATOR BIAS CONTROL WHEEL & INDICATOR
46	COMPASS CARD HOLDER
47	HYDRAULIC HAND PUMP
48	COCKPIT HEATING CONTROL
49	AIR BOTTLE INFLATION VALVE
50	HOOD JETTISON LEVER

PORT COCKPIT

Above and opposite: Port and starboard sides of the cockpit interior from the Prototype Notes. *(Jet Age Museum Collection)*

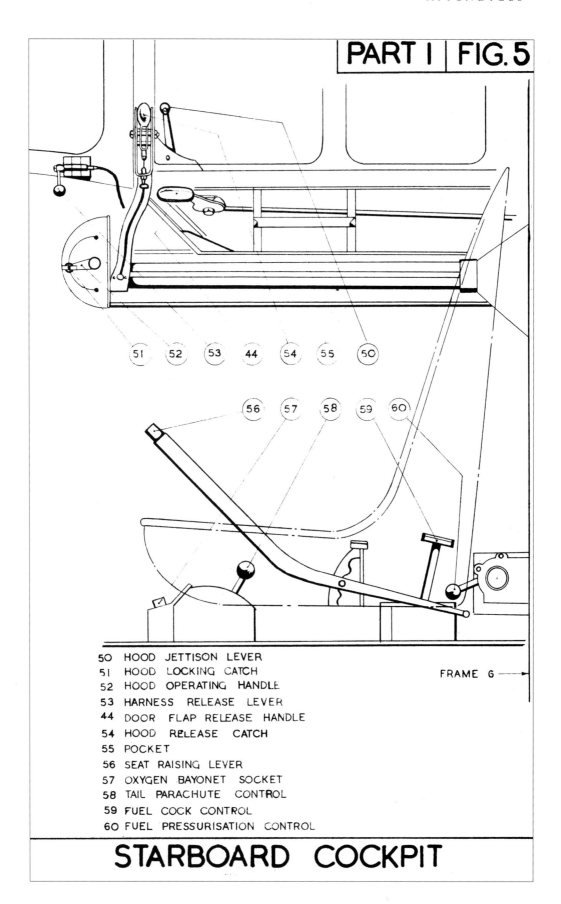

PART I | FIG.5

50 HOOD JETTISON LEVER
51 HOOD LOCKING CATCH
52 HOOD OPERATING HANDLE
53 HARNESS RELEASE LEVER
44 DOOR FLAP RELEASE HANDLE
54 HOOD RELEASE CATCH
55 POCKET
56 SEAT RAISING LEVER
57 OXYGEN BAYONET SOCKET
58 TAIL PARACHUTE CONTROL
59 FUEL COCK CONTROL
60 FUEL PRESSURISATION CONTROL

FRAME 6

STARBOARD COCKPIT

C   BILL BALDWIN'S INSTRUMENT LIST

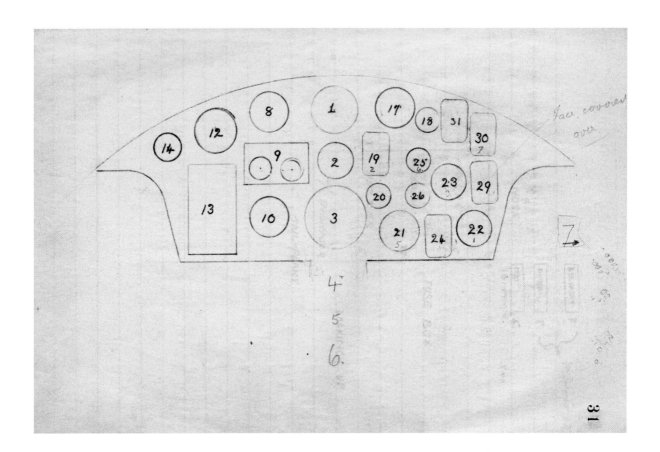

Sketch of the E28's instrument layout from the notes which Bill Baldwin kept during its construction. The instruments are listed in the accompanying text in the order in which they appear in his notes. (*Jet Age Museum Collection*)

Drawing Z28196, issue E:

1   Artificial horizon. Smith Mk II. Removed
2   Altimeter. SS&S Mk XIVA. Broken
3   Turn indicator. R&S Ltd Mk IA. Removed 4 July 1941
5   Compass. P8. Broken 26 April 1941
6   Brake pressure. Dunlop triple reading
8   Air speed indicator. SS&S Mk IXF to 480mph
9   Oxygen regulator. L. Adams Mk VIIIA
10   Fuel contents. 0–80 gallons
12   Undercarriage indicator. Air Comp Ltd
4   Burner pressure. Barnet Mk IA
17   Engine speed indicator. Record Electrical Co. Ltd. 2,000 to 20,000 rev.
26   Radiator temperature thermometer. The British Rotothermo Co. Ltd Mk VIIIH. 40°–140°C. Removed
19   Compressor delivery. S&M Mk XIC. 0–100lb/sq in. Broken
20   Fuel pressure. Barnet Inst Mk IA. 0–500lb/sq in
21   Engine com pressure. SS&S Mk IXF
22   Temp thermo. Mk I. Exhaust 0°–700°C
23   Ditto. Sangamo Weston Ltd Mk I. Compressor delivery 0°–350°C. Removed from panel 20 February 1941.

25 Ditto. N&Z Mk III. Engine compartment. −30° +50°C. November 1940
31 Ditto. CI Co. Ltd Mk IA. Oil 0°–100°C
24 Pressure. KG London. Turbine exhaust 0–10lb/sq in
29 Oil pressure. S&M Mk IXC. 0–100lb/sq in
30 Oil Pressure. N&Z Mk VIIIA. 0–5lb/sq in
18 Air temp thermo. N&Z Mk III. −30° to +50°C
14 Hydraulic pressure. Mk ID. 0–3,000lb/sq in. Removed
–   Pressure gauge. On emergency air bottle
–   Brake pressure. Dunlop. Single. 0–350lb/sq in
2   Altimeter. Mk XIV. 1,000–35,000ft. Removed 14 May 1941
19 Compressor delivery. S&M Mk XIC. 0–100lb/sq in
14 Hyd pressure. Mk ID. 0–3,000lb/sq in
5   Compass. P8
1   Artificial horizon. Mk IIX. Removed 4 July 1941
2   Altimeter. Mk XIVA

D   THE CRANWELL FLIGHTS

E28/39N W4041: Times taken at Cranwell by Bill Baldwin:

14 May
Engine run only, 2053 to 2058 (5 minutes). Taxiing 2110 to 2135 (25 minutes).

15 May
1st flight. Engine on 1920. Take off 1940. Landed 1957. Engine off 2003. Engine time 43 minutes. Flying time 17 minutes.
After 1st flight: starboard radiator blanked off for all further flights; new switch fitted to port undercarriage down lock; pressure in nose wheel leg 115lb/sq in; pressure in nose wheel tyre 20lb/sq in.

16 May
Engine run only, 1256 to 1258 (2 minutes).
2nd flight. Engine on 1315. Take off 1325. Landed 1349. Engine off 1355. Engine time 40 minutes. Flying time 24 minutes.
After 2nd flight: fuel pressure adjusted; cooling system: 30 per cent glycol and 70 per cent water.
3rd flight. Engine on 1858. Take off 1911. Landed 1943. Engine off 1950. Engine time 52 minutes. Flying time 32 minutes.
4th flight. Engine on 2024. Take off 2032. Landed 2118. Engine off 2124. Engine time 60 minutes. Flying time 46 minutes.
After 4th flight: port undercarriage leg ram refilled with oil; elevator controls adjusted; undercarriage doors adjusted.

17 May
Engine run only, 1612 to 1616 (4 minutes).
5th flight. Engine on 1636. Take off 1645. Landed 1719. Engine off 1725. Engine time 49 minutes. Flying time 34 minutes. Engine stopped

on runway by Mr Sayer. Taxied from runway to hangar by Flt Lt Johnstone [of Power Jets], 1745 to 1755 (10 minutes).

6th flight. Engine on 1858. Take off 1905. Landed 1933. Engine off 1936. Engine time 38 minutes. Flying time 28 minutes.

7th flight. Engine on 2000. Take off 2009. Landed 2058. Engine off 2103. Engine time 63 minutes. Flying time 49 minutes.

After 7th flight: starboard undercarriage wheel replaced (tyre damaged); port undercarriage ram replaced; oxygen bottle fitted and system tested.

18 May

8th flight. Engine on 1514. Plane moved off 1517. Take off 1519. Landed 1615. Engine off 1617. Engine time 63 minutes. Flying time 56 minutes.

After 8th flight: 8-inch trimmer cord on top face of port aileron.

9th flight. Engine on 1855. Plane moved off 1858. Take off 1901. Landed 1957. Engine stopped 1958. Engine time 63 minutes. Flying time 56 minutes.

After 9th flight: 8-inch trimmer cord added to top face of port aileron; 6-inch trimmer cord on top and bottom faces of port and starboard elevator; support bracket fitted to throttle switch; new operating arm fitted to port and starboard undercarriage down lock switch; oxygen bottle replaced.

20 May

Engine run only, 1012 to 1014 (2 minutes), 1019 to 1021 (2 minutes), 1031 to 1033 (2 minutes), 1043 to 1045 (2 minutes).

Emergency bottle air pressure increased to 900lb/sq in; accumulator charged and re-fitted.

21 May

10th flight. Engine on 1234. Plane moved off 1237. Take off 1240. Landed 1255. Engine off 1255. Engine time 21 minutes. Flying time 15 minutes. Tyre burst when landing on runway. Port undercarriage wheel replaced on flying field. Taxied from runway to hangar by Flt Lt Johnstone, 1329 to 1335 (6 minutes).

11th flight. Engine on 1805. Plane moved off 1807. Take off 1813. Landed 1825. Engine off 1827. Engine time 22 minutes. Flying time 12 minutes.

After 11th flight: 3-inch trimmer cord removed from port aileron.

22 May

12th flight. Engine on 1033. Plane moved off 1036. Take off 1044. Landed 1130. Engine off 1136. Engine time 63 minutes. Flying time 46 minutes.

After 12th flight: 4-inch trimmer cord on port and starboard faces of rudder.

13th flight. Engine on 1205. Plane moved off 1206. Take off 1208. Landed 1250. Engine off 1254. Engine time 49 minutes. Flying time 42 minutes.

After 13th flight: 2-inch trimmer cord added to top face of port aileron; port undercarriage wheel removed, brake drum checked and wheel replaced; nose wheel leg pressure checked; 9-inch trimmer cord added to port and starboard elevator top and bottom faces; port and starboard ailerons adjusted to give $\frac{3}{16}$ inch droop.

27 May

14th flight. Engine on 1404. Plane moved off 1405. Take off 1411. Landed 1437. Engine off 1439. Engine time 35 minutes. Flying time 26 minutes.
15th flight. Engine on 1838. Plane moved off 1838. Take off 1840. Landed 1922. Engine off 1927. Engine time 49 minutes. Flying time 42 minutes.
After 15th flight: port sight feed glass cracked.

28 May

Engine run only, 1053 to 1056 (3 minutes).
16th flight. Engine on 1117. Plane moved off 1118. Take off 1121. Landed 1212. Engine off 1214. Engine time 57 minutes. Flying time 51 minutes.
17th flight. Engine on 1600. Plane moved off 1602. Take off 1604. Landed and engine off 1656. Engine time 56 minutes. Flying time 52 minutes. Engine stopped in flight and failed to start. Emergency used for nose wheel.

Total engine time 14 hours 46 minutes. Total flying time 10 hours 28 minutes. Total fuel used 1,058 gallons.

E   CAMOUFLAGE AND MARKINGS

Taxiing Trials, April 1941

W4041 had a bare metal finish, except for fabric covering on all five control surfaces (rudder, elevators and ailerons). The colour of the fabric covering is not recorded. It could have been red oxide or grey primer; it looks too dark in the photographs to be a silver dope finish. There is a narrow strip along each side of the fuselage with groups of five vertical lines of thermal paint at approximately 1 foot intervals. No wireless aerial was fitted and there was no serial number or any other marking.

The Cranwell Flights, May 1941

The standard trainer scheme was specified for experimental and prototype aircraft early in the war: Dark Green and Dark Earth camouflage on upper surfaces with Yellow undersides. These were the colours worn by the E28 when it first flew at Cranwell in May 1941. The actual camouflage pattern is not known.

The only known photograph (see p. 41) of the E28's first Cranwell flight, a poor-quality still from the ciné-film taken by Michael Daunt in the absence of any official photographer, shows a large type A1 roundel on the fuselage side, probably of 35in diameter including the outer yellow ring, and a non-standard fin flash some 30in high with equal divisions of red, white and blue. Although not visible in the photo, it presumably also had the serial W4041/G painted in 8-in black letters and numbers behind the fuselage roundel, 30-in type B red and blue roundels on the upper wing surfaces, and type A red, white and blue roundels under the wings.

The finish would have been matt overall. Although the yellow P in a circle fuselage marking for experimental and prototype aircraft was specified in early 1940, the E28 is not wearing it in this photograph.

Farnborough, 1942–5

We are on more certain ground with the E28's camouflage and markings during its period of flight testing at Farnborough. It is a 1942-type scheme, and although it is not clear when it was applied it is believed to have been done before W4041 went to Farnborough, where it first flew on 20 December of that year. The same scheme was almost certainly worn by W4046.

The E28 retained the yellow undersurfaces, while the upper surfaces were now in the new standard colours of dark green and ocean grey. The fuselage roundel is now type C1 of 18-in diameter, with narrow 1-in thick white and yellow rings, while the 2-in thick, 16-in yellow P is in a 1-in thick, 27-in diameter circle. The fin flash, too, has a narrow central white area and is 24in high. Upper wing roundels are still type B, but underwing roundels are the new type C (with the narrow white ring) of 17-in diameter. Most of the pattern of the camouflage is shown in many photos, and it seems to accord with the pattern which the E28 still wears today.

The inside of the air intake at the nose was bare metal, except for the outer rim, where the exterior colours turned in for an inch or so. The cockpit was painted in the standard interior green, with the instrument panel mid-tan brown in colour.

Science Museum, 1946 to Present

The E28 made its last flight on 20 February 1945, at Farnborough. By the time it was installed in the Science Museum some fourteen months later it had been repainted, with a shinier finish, in a scheme in which it never flew.

It retains the fuselage roundel, P and serial, the fin flash and the upper wing roundels of its Farnborough scheme, but the upper surfaces have been repainted in dark green and dark earth, its pre-Farnborough colours. Large type A, pre-Farnborough roundels of 35-in diameter have been painted on the undersurfaces of the wings. The legend 'THE GLOSTER E28/39' has been neatly signwritten on each side of the nose.

F   PLANS AND MODELS

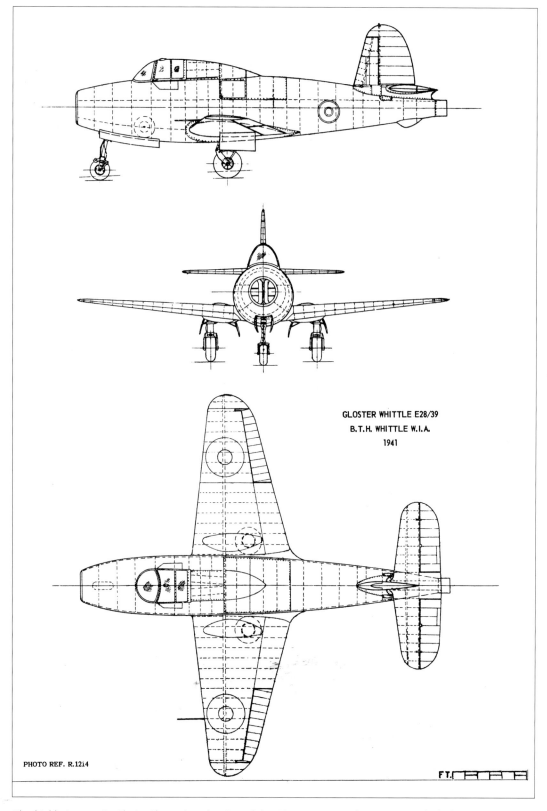

GLOSTER WHITTLE E28/39
B.T.H. WHITTLE W.I.A.
1941

PHOTO REF. R.1214

FT.

The highly inaccurate Gloster three-view drawing of the E28, company ref. R1214, on which the Frog 1/72 scale model of 1966 was based. *(Jet Age Museum Collection)*

Acquiring good scale drawings of the E28 has been a problem over the years. Models of the aircraft have suffered accordingly. The problem began in 1945 with the publication of Owen Thetford's *Aircraft of the Fighting Powers*, volume 6 (Harborough), which included the first three-view plans of the E28 to be made public. Although reasonably accurate in detail, they included major errors: the span was shown about 9in too big, while the fuselage was shown as a whopping 45in too long: it had been drawn at a scale of approximately 1/63 instead of the quoted 1/72.

Gloster issued its own 1/72 scale three-view (see previous page), which was identical to the Harborough version except that it did not include fuselage and wing cross-sections. The company gave it the title 'Gloster Whittle E28/39 BTH Whittle W1A 1941' and it also carried the words 'Photo Ref R1214'. It is not clear whether Harborough based their drawings on the company version or vice versa.

These drawings formed the basis for the first plastic model kit of the E28, issued by Frog in their 1/72 scale Trailblazers series in 1966. *Meccano Magazine* editor J.D. McHard, writing in *Aeromodeller* in September that year, wrote 'something very nasty happened to the fuselage of the Frog Gloster Whittle now – at last – in the shops. Reliance on drawings supplied by the manufacturers without careful checking has resulted in a grotesquely oversize fuselage. Scale modellers be warned – again – maker's drawings are usually the worst available!' Generations of modelmakers assumed that the model was reasonably accurate and gained a false impression of the E28 as a large, barrel-like fuselage perched on undersized wings when the real thing was altogether smaller and neater. The kit was later reissued by the Russian manufacturer Novo and can also be found under the Eastern Express or Chematic label.

The company's more detailed GA drawings and the plans in its secret 'Prototype Notes', both reproduced in this book, are not generally available. The first accurate drawings to be published were by James Goulding, who had worked in the Gloster design office under Carter, later becoming a distinguished aviation historian and illustrator. His drawings

A simple but accurate kit of the E28 in 1/72 scale is Greg Meggs's High Planes kit from Australia.

Gloster E28/39 "Whittle"
Britain's first jet aircraft

HIGH PLANES MODELS

Australian made

1/72 limited run injection moulded kit

and article in *Aircraft Illustrated* in November 1969 got it right. He had seen the actual E28 himself and his article includes what is still the most authoritative colour information available.

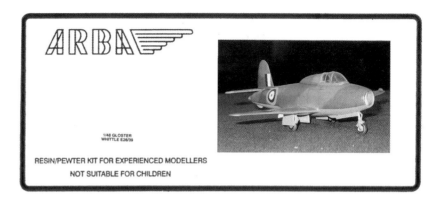

It was not until 1990 that Barrie Hygate published his classic *British Experimental Jet Aircraft*, which included pretty much all available external information on the E28 in an accurate five-view drawing. This seems to have been the basis for Greg Meggs's 1/72 High Planes injection moulded kit. Arba's 1/48 resin kit of the E28 is based on another good set of drawings by James Kightly, published in 1992 in Mike Chilestone's splendid *Gloster Meteor and E28/39 Pioneer* (Mushroom Model Guide no. 1). At the time of going to press, a new kit of the E28, from Special Hobby, was about to be released.

Another accurate model, this time in 1/48 scale, can be made from Arba's resin and pewter kit, mastered by Alan Ranger and Bill Anderson. Both this and the High Planes kit were available at the time of writing.

The striking box art for a new 1/48 scale injection-moulded kit of the E28 released in January 2004 by Special Hobby of the Czech Republic. *(Special Hobby)*

There is still a pitfall for the unwary, though. The length of the E28 is usually quoted as 25ft 3.75in. This figure is taken from the length of 25ft 3.7in given in the frames diagram in the 'Prototype Notes', but a closer look reveals that this is the length of the fuselage monocoque excluding

canopy injected

the jet pipe, the length of which was not the same throughout the E28's career.

Other plans include inaccurate ones by Chris Bowley, published in *Aviation News* in August 1991 and *Airfix Magazine* the following November.

G   THE MISSING E28 RECORDS

When it became clear that the Gloster Company's days were numbered, chief designer Richard Walker asked one of the staff, John Carter, to compile a company history. It was the first systematic attempt to make as complete a record as possible of the Gloster story.

'This book was compiled by me while in the service of the Gloster Aircraft Co. from various records and cuttings,' Carter wrote in 1986. A copy was deposited in the Gloucestershire County Record Office in 1965 (Ref. D1247) and there are still a few copies in private hands. Miraculously, the original part-manuscript part-typescript has reappeared and is now in Jet Age Museum's archives – it was saved from a skip by Harry Holmes, a former public relations officer at British Aerospace, Woodford, and passed to Manchester Museum of Science & Industry, which donated it to Jet Age Museum in 1997. In it John Carter lists all the documents available to him when he was compiling his history. The following is his list of records relating to the E28. Jet Age Museum would be pleased to hear from anyone who knows of their current whereabouts, if indeed they have survived.

Envelope no. 20 containing: Remarks by P. Sayer, Extracts from letter Air Com Sir F. Whittle, Photographs, Design Certificate, Reports on flights, Schedule of flight trials, Reports of Design Meetings, Report of examination of a/c.

Albums of Photographs 9A.

Folders: 2C (Stressing assumptions), 3C (Model tests), 4C (Reports of visits), 5C (Correspondence to June 1940), 6C (Correspondence to May 1940), 7C (Jet pipe lagging), 8C (Fuel tanks), 9C (Weights & CG), 10C (type record), 11C (Prototype Notes), 12C (Leading particulars), 13C (Design Meetings), 14C (General Design Data), 15C (Prototype Notes), 16C (Tricycle u/c), 17C (Maintenance notes) and 28C (Addendum to type record).

BIBLIOGRAPHY

BOOKS

Barnes, C.H., *Shorts Aircraft since 1900*, London, Putnam, 2nd edn with new material by D. James, 1989

Blackmore, L.K., *Hawker*, Shrewsbury, Airlife, 1993

Brown, E., *Wings of the Weird and Wonderful*, Shrewsbury, Airlife, 1983

Bulman, G.P., *An Account of Partnership: Industry, Government and the Aero Engine*, Rolls-Royce Heritage Trust Historical Series, no. 31, Derby, 2001

Chilestone, M., *Gloster Meteor and E28/39 Pioneer*, Mushroom Model Guide, no. 1, Nottingham, Mushroom Model Publications [1996]

Dennis, R., *Farnborough's Jets*, Fleet, Footmark, 1999

Ethell, J. and Price A., *World War II Fighting Jets*, Shrewsbury, Airlife, 1994

Foxworth, T.G., *The Speed Seekers*, London, Macdonald & Jane's, 1975

Fozard, J.W. (ed.), *Sydney Camm and the Hurricane*, Shrewsbury, Airlife, 1991

Golley, J., *Whittle: The True Story*, Shrewsbury, Airlife, 1987

Goulding, J., 'Founding the Jet Fighter Era at Glosters', in M. Horseman (ed.), *Aircraft Illustrated Annual 1980*, Shepperton, Ian Allan, 1979

——, *Interceptor*, London, Ian Allan, 1986

Granger, A., *Hawker Woodcock Danecock Series (Data Plan Number 1)*, Oxford, Taurus, 1973

Grierson, J., *Through Russia by Air*, London, G.T. Foulis, 1933

——, *Jet Flight*, London, Sampson Low Marston [1946]

Gunston, B., *Fedden: The Life of Sir Roy Fedden*, Rolls-Royce Heritage Trust Historical Series, no. 26, Derby, 1998

Henshaw, A., *Sigh for a Merlin*, London, John Murray, 1979, and Hamlyn, 1980

Hygate, B., *British Experimental Jet Aircraft*, Hemel Hempstead, Argus, 1990

Jackson, A.J., *De Havilland Aircraft since 1909*, 3rd edn revised by R.T. Jackson, London, Putnam, 1987

James, D.N., *Gloster Aircraft since 1917*, 2nd edn, London, Putnam, 1987

Jefford, C.G., *RAF Squadrons*, Shrewsbury, Airlife, 1988

Lewis, P., *The British Bomber since 1914*, 2nd edn, London, Putnam, 1975

Lumsden, A. and Thetford O., *On Silver Wings*, London, Osprey 1993

Mason, F.K., *Hawker Aircraft since 1920*, 3rd edn, London, Putnam, 1991

——, *The British Fighter since 1912*, London, Putnam, 1992

——, *The British Bomber since 1914*, London, Putnam, 1994

Matthews, H., *Gloster-Whittle E28/39 Pioneer: A Flying Chronology*, X-Planes Profile, no. 3, Beirut, 2001

Meekcoms, K.J. and Morgan, E.B., *The British Aircraft Specifications File*, Tonbridge, Air-Britain, 1994

Middleton, D., *Test Pilots: The Story of British Test Flying, 1903–1984*, London, Willow (William Collins), 1985

Munson, K., *Fighters Between the Wars 1919–39* London, Blandford, 1970

——, *Bombers Between the Wars 1919–39*. London, Blandford, 1970

Penrose, H., *British Aviation: The Adventuring Years 1920–1929*, London, Putnam, 1973

——, *British Aviation: Widening Horizons 1930–1934*, London, HMSO, 1979

——, *British Aviation: The Ominous Skies 1935–1939*, London, HMSO, 1980

Philpott, B., *Meteor*, Wellingborough, Patrick Stephens, 1986

Rennison, J., *Wings Over Gloucestershire*, 2nd edn, Stroud, Aspect, 2000

Ritchie, S., *Industry and Air Power: The Expansion of British Aircraft Production, 1935–1941*, London, Frank Cass, 1997

Robertson, B., *Sopwith: The Man and his Aircraft*, Letchworth, Air Review, 1970

Shacklady, E., *The Gloster Meteor*, London, Macdonald, 1962

Sinnott, C., *The Royal Air Force and Aircraft Design, 1923–1939: Air Staff Operational Requirements*, London, Frank Cass, 2001

Smith, G.G., *Gas Turbines and Jet Propulsion for Aircraft*, 4th edn, London, Flight, 1946

Taylor, J.W.R., Taylor, M.J.H. and Mondey D., *The Guinness Book of Air Facts and Feats*, Enfield, Guinness Superlatives, 1973

Thetford, O., *Aircraft of the Fighting Powers*, vol. 6, Leicester, Harborough, 1945

Thompson, D. and Sturtivant, R., *Royal Air Force Aircraft J1–J9999*, Tonbridge, Air Britain, 1987

Walker, R., *The Jet Age*, London, News Chronicle, 1952

Waterton, W.A., *The Quick and the Dead*, London, Frederick Muller, 1956

PRESS ARTICLES AND CORRESPONDENCE

Birtles, P., 'DH77 Interceptor', *Aeroplane Monthly*, April 1977

——, 'Troublesome Trimotors', *Aeroplane Monthly*, May 1979

Bowley, C. 'E28/39 Plans', *Aviation News*, 16–29 August 1991

——, 'E28/39 plans', *Airfix Magazine*, November 1991

Butler, P. 'The Gloster E28/39', *Aero Militaria* (Air Britain), Spring 2001

Buttler, T., 'UK Jet Pioneers', *Air Enthusiast*, May/June and July/August 2003

Carter, W.G., *Flight*, 27 October 1949

Daily Telegraph, London, obituary of Sir Frank Whittle, 10 August 1996

Feilden, R., 'The Contribution of Power Jets Ltd to Jet Propulsion', *Journal of the Royal Aeronautical Society*, February 1993

Gloucestershire Aviation Collection, 'I Saw Whittle Hop the First Jet', *GAC News*, no. 20, January 1999

Gloucestershire Echo, 'Death of Mr W. Carter', 4 March 1969

Golley, J., 'The Whittle Revolution', *Aeroplane Monthly*, June 1991

Goulding, J., 'The Gloster E28/39: Britain's First Jet Plane', *Aircraft Illustrated*, November 1969

Gunston, B., 'Dawn of the Jet Age', *Aeroplane Monthly*, April 1977

——, 'Database: Early Jet Aircraft', *Aeroplane*, May 2001

Hilton, W.F., 'British Aeronautical Research Facilities', *Journal of the Royal Aeronautical Society*, centenary issue, January 1966

McHard, J.D., 'Scale comments', *Aeromodeller*, September 1966

Sampson, A., 'Cosy Cottage Home of Test-Flight Hero', *Gloucestershire Echo*, 19 January 1991

Skeet, T., 'Meteor Momentum', *Aeroplane*, April 2003

Sunday Express, 'Jet Pioneer Now a Pony and Trap Man', 15 May 1966

The Times, London, Obituary of W.G. Carter, 1 March 1969

Whittle, F., *Flight*, 27 October 1949

——, 'How Jets Developed', letter in the *Daily Telegraph*, 13 March 1962

UNPUBLISHED MATERIAL

Baldwin, B., Documents and papers presented to Jet Age Museum in 1998

Brown, E.M., Presentation to Whittle Reactionaries at Institute of Mechanical

Engineers, London, 16 December 1998. Video of the event presented to Jet Age Museum by Sqn Ldr Geoffrey Bone, January 2001

Burroughes, H., Lecture given to the Royal Aeronautical Society, Cheltenham and Gloucester branch, at Wheatstone Hall, Gloucester, on 12 January 1967

Carter, J.H., 'History of Gloster Aircraft', draft donated to Jet Age Museum in 1997

Cuss, J.F., Papers presented to Jet Age Museum in 1995

Fielding, B., 'Life with the GAC: A Look into the Past as Remembered by Baz': Memoirs, photographs and press cuttings deposited with Jet Age Museum in 1995

Gillett, S., 'The Aircraft Industry in Avon and Gloucestershire', Ironbridge Institute, Master of Social Science (Industrial Heritage) course dissertation, 1999

Hill, S.H., 'The Early History of Gas Turbine Jet Propulsion for Flight', 1974, in the Jet Age Museum Collection

Summers, M., with Aves, A., 'Life, Luck and Love: Tales of an International Test Pilot', privately printed autobiography presented to Jet Age Museum by the author in July 1995

Walker, R.W., Documents and Notes (Private Collection)

NATIONAL ARCHIVE, OFFICIAL AND COMPANY DOCUMENTS

AIR 20/1783, Air Ministry minute from CAS, 16 October 1942

AIR 62/40, 'Gloster High Speed Aircraft', 1939

AIR 62/606, Frank Whittle, History of E28

AVIA 15/310, W.G.A. Perring and A.A. Hall, Note on the development of jet propelled aeroplanes

AVIA 15/310, W.S. Farren to W.G. Carter, 17 April 1940

AVIA 15/310, W.S. Farren to DGRD, Gloster Whittle development, 10 May 1940

AVIA 15/461, Deputy Director of Technical Development to OC RAF Cranwell, 28 April 1941

AVIA 15/461, P.B. Walker, Note on Gloster Whittle project, 19 February 1941.

AVIA 15/461, Visit of US Government representatives to Gloster Aircraft Co., 28 July 1941

AVIA 15/974, H.T. Tizard, minute 22 on file SB4105, Technical discussions on Gloster Whittle developments

AVIA 15/974, DDSR1 to Sir Henry Tizard, 31 January 1941

AVIA 15/975, DD/RDA, Notes on visit to Gloster Aircraft Co. Ltd on 16 June 1942, Discussion with Mr Carter and other members of the firm's staff

AVIA 15/975, J.H. Larrard, AD/ADI: production capacity for (F9/40) Meteor, Report of visit to Gloster, 24 June 1942

AVIA 15/976, Notes on RAE letter, 10 February 1943

AVIA 15/976, H.J. Allwright, Gloster F9/40, 1 April 1943

AVIA 15/1708, Future gas turbine aircraft projects, Discussion on 8 June 1942

AVIA 15/1923, Lord Beaverbrook to Gloster, 9 January 1941

AVIA 15/3922, Gloster high-speed research aircraft, Whittle engine installation, Notes on the design and sketches of schemes I and II

'E28/39 Prototype Notes', Gloster Aircraft Co. Ltd, December 1942

'WG Carter CBE FRAeS', Obituary and tribute issued by Hawker Siddeley Aviation Ltd [March 1969]

WEBSITES

411 Squadron RAF: escort for E28.
www.holoduke.com/411%20ARS/the_war_years/pages/secret_mission.htm

ALLSTAR network: Sir Sydney Camm. www.allstar.fiu.edu/aero/camm.htm

Andy's Austin Seven Page: Article from Douglas Ormrod of Auckland, New Zealand. www.geocities.com/MotorCity/4752/articles.html

Bedfordshire County Council: Guide to Collections: Business Records. www.bedfordshire.gov.uk/Bedscc/SDCountryrec.nsf/Web%5CThe Page/ Guide+to+Collections:+Business+Records

Brief History of Bedfordshire. www.kbnet.co.uk/brianp/history.html

The Sir Frank Whittle Commemorative Group. www.whittle-lutterworth.com

Gloucestershire Portal: Wilfred George Carter OBE, Aircraft Designer. www.softdata.co.uk/gloucester/carter.htm

INDEX

Illustrations in **bold**

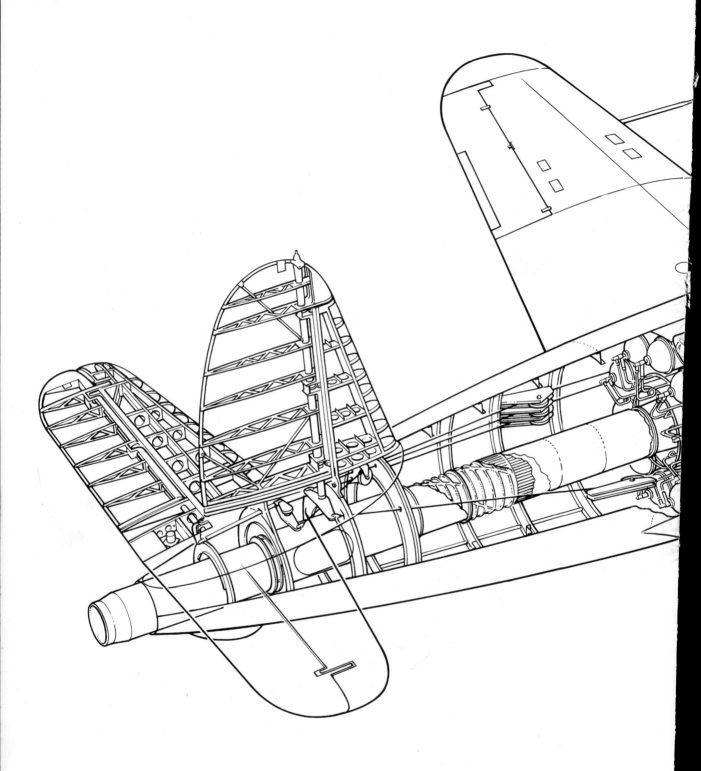